Decorating
Fabric

Decorating Fabric

Print, stencil, paint and dye
100 inspirational projects

Susie Stokoe

LORENZ BOOKS

First published in 2001 by Lorenz Books

Lorenz Books
is an imprint of
Anness Publishing Limited
Hermes House
88–89 Blackfriars Road
London SE1 8HA

This edition distributed in Canada by Raincoast Books,
9050 Shaughnessy Street, Vancouver, British Columbia V6P 6E5

Published in the USA by Lorenz Books, Anness Publishing Inc.,
27 West 20th Street, New York, NY 10011

A CIP catalogue record for this book is available
from the British Library

Publisher Joanna Lorenz
Managing Editor Helen Suddell
Project Editor Simona Hill
Designer Jane Coney
Editorial Reader Richard McGinlay
Production Controller Wendy Lawson

10 9 8 7 6 5 4 3 2 1

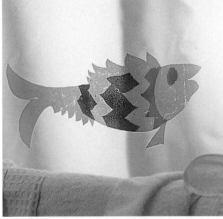

A few basic safety rules should be followed when working with dyes. Label all solutions and keep them away from children and animals. Do not eat or drink while using dyes, and wash your hands before handling food. If you spill dye powder, sweep up as much as possible before washing with plenty of water. Blot up spilt dye solution with newspaper, then wash down. Remove dye stains from hard surfaces with household cleaner or diluted bleach.

Contents

Introduction

Decorating fabric with an assortment of paints, inks and dyes is fun to do, and creating unique and original fashion accessories and soft furnishings is

satisfying and rewarding. As well as explaining and

illustrating all the different techniques, this book contains 100 step-by-step projects ranging from simple to complex and from small to large. You can begin in Chapter 1 with a leaf print or ready-made stamp design and progress to the more ambitious skills of batik and space-dyeing, following the symbols that indicate which projects are easy or more time-consuming to make. The symbol ⌁ indicates a project is relatively straightforward to do and that a complete beginner could tackle it with ease. Projects with the symbol ⌁⌁⌁⌁⌁ indicate that an advanced level of skill and knowledge is required to complete the project.

If you are artistic, you may want to draw your own designs freehand, but if not, there are plenty of templates to trace or enlarge on a photo-copier to the size required. Some of the most striking designs are the simplest; for example, using masking tape or ruled lines to create a bold geometric grid. The charm of hand-

made fabrics is their spontaneity, so do not worry too much about perfection.

If you are unsure of your skills, practise on a piece of spare fabric first or dye

several pieces of fabric in a dye bath and choose the best to assemble the

project. Remnants and test pieces can be made into small gifts such as a pretty headband or lavender bag.

The Projects

Printing and
Stencilling

Printing your own patterns gives a very special, hand-crafted look, with much more character than the perfect repetition of machine-produced textiles. This chapter shows you the many different techniques — traditional stencils, wooden blocks and lino cuts, sponge and foam, natural objects such as fruit, feathers and leaves, and modern ready-made stamps.

Fresh Impressions

Hand-printing fabric is a traditional technique still practised in many parts of the world today. In the 19th century, William Morris and the Arts and Crafts Movement revived hand block-printing on textiles and wallpaper, creating a new fashion in interior design that has continued to the present day. As well as using hand-carved printing blocks, Morris also re-introduced natural vegetable dyes such as indigo and madder, which had been replaced by the harsh colours of chemical dyes. Today we are lucky that so many subtle shades of specially designed fabric paints and inks are widely available for use on a variety of fabric types.

The great charm of hand printing is that each print is slightly different, depending on how much paint or ink you use and how much pressure you apply. If you want your design to look uniform throughout, use fresh paint or ink for each impression and maintain an even rhythm — it helps to practise first until you get the "feel" of the technique, whether it is stencilling, stamping or

using a potato cut. Alternatively, you can deliberately exploit the special qualities of hand printing and apply fresh ink or paint less often, so that the colour is slightly uneven. This approach works particularly well when you are imitating nature, for example a pattern of leaves, because no two leaves are the same colour. Stand back from your work from time to time to check that the over-all effect is balanced.

Experiment with negative prints and stencils – using light-coloured ink or paint on dark fabric. If you are making a set of cushions or bed linen, it is very effective to mix-and-match positive and

negative versions of the same print. The great advantage of creating your own fabric is that you decide what you want to do, and modern photocopiers have made enlarging or reducing an image very simple. Many printing and stencilling designs can be printed on walls and wood as well as on fabrics, so you can achieve a completely co-ordinated effect throughout a whole room.

The materials you choose to work with – the types of paint and the fabric weave – will affect the density of colour on the finished design. Choose appropriately using the instructions as a guide.

Materials

Image-transfer cream

Using this technique, you print or stamp patterns on paper, then cut them out and transfer them on to fabric. The images are fixed (set) with an iron, following the manufacturer's instructions. This technique works well with photocopied images, which can be enlarged or reduced.

Metallic powders

Added to a fabric-painting medium, metallic powders give a glittery effect with a hard-wearing finish.

Printing materials

Leaves and feathers make beautiful prints. Potato prints are always successful, and fruits can also be cut in half to serve as blocks.

Ready-made stamps

Stamps mounted on small blocks are available in thousands of designs.

Sponge or foam

Different types give different results. Close-density is best for detailed motifs and gives a smooth, sharp print. Medium- and low-density creates a more textured effect.

Spray adhesive (stencil mount)

Spray on to stencils to hold them temporarily in place. Always use in a well-ventilated room.

Fabrics

Natural fabrics such as cotton, linen, muslin (cheesecloth) and velvet are the best to use, since they absorb colour easily. Pre-wash the fabric, and don't use fabric conditioner or starch. Avoid fabrics that are loosely woven, furry, or have treated surfaces.

Protect the work surface with a backing cloth, and insert cardboard inside pillowcases and cushion covers to prevent the colour from spreading through to the other side.

Fabric inks

Permanent fabric inks are available in a huge range of colours either in inkpad form or in applicator bottles.

Fabric paints

There is a wide range of permanent paints specially designed for use on fabrics. Many are fixed (set) by ironing the fabric on the reverse side with a warm dry iron. Protect the ironing board with kitchen paper or layers of brown paper and newspaper.

You will need different equipment for different techniques, but some basic tools will be useful whatever printing or stencilling method you choose to use.

Equipment

Masking tape

Use temporarily to mask off straight lines, and to hold stencils in place.

Needles

Use to add decorative surface stitches to fabric. Large needles can be used to transfer a design by pricking it out.

Paint rollers

Various sizes in sponge or foam, are used to ink stamps and apply paint.

Plate or palette

Use to hold ink or paint, and to mix different colours.

Ruler or tape measure

Use to plan out a large design and to make accurate measurements on cardboard, paper and fabric.

Scissors

Use dressmaker's scissors for cutting fabric, and paper scissors for paper.

Stencil card/Mylar film

Special waxed stencil card will last longer than ordinary cardboard. Cut stencils out using a craft knife and work on a cutting mat. Use to make stencils that will have repeat usage.

Tracing paper

Use to trace templates and to transfer designs from paper to cardboard.

Brushes

Use as specified in each project. Use a separate brush to apply glue or varnish and always clean thoroughly.

Craft knife

Use a sharp-bladed craft knife to cut stamps and stencils. Use a cutting mat to protect the work surface.

Dressmaker's pins

Use to temporarily hold pieces of fabric together.

Fabric markers

Use a soft pencil to trace templates. Felt-tipped pens and marker pens are used to draw designs on to paper or medium- to low-density sponge. Special markers are used for temporarily marking fabric.

Linoleum and lino-cutting tools

Linoleum (lino) is available from craft suppliers. Use special lino-cutting tools to scoop out unwanted areas from the design.

Rubber stamps are widely available in many craft and department stores, but it is much more rewarding to make your own printing block using one of the following simple techniques.

Techniques

Polystyrene (styrofoam)

This is easy to cut and gives good clean edges. Always mount it on to hardboard before cutting your design.

You will need

sheet of polystyrene (styrofoam),
approximately 1cm/½in thick
piece of hardboard, the same size as
the polystyrene
wood glue or PVA (white) glue
felt-tipped pen
craft knife

1 Stick the polystyrene and hardboard backing together, using wood glue or PVA (white) glue. Without waiting for the glue to set, draw a design with a felt-tipped pen. The pattern will be reversed when printed.

2 Cut around the outline of the design using a sharp craft knife. If this is done before the glue has set, these pieces will pull away easily. Remove unwanted pieces of polystyrene as you cut them out.

3 Make shallow, angular cuts to scoop out the details. Use a new blade for this, so that the cuts are sharp and you do not accidentally lift pieces that are only partially separated.

Potato prints

Most of us learn this technique as school children, but potato prints are amazingly effective and should not be overlooked.

You will need

medium-sized raw potato
sharp kitchen knife
fine felt-tipped pen
craft knife

1 Make a single cut right through the middle of the potato, using a sharp kitchen knife. This will give a smooth surface for printing.

2 Draw the motif on the sliced potato using a fine felt-tipped pen. The design will be reversed when printed.

3 Use a craft knife to cut the outline, then undercut and scoop out the background. Cut out any details.

Foam

High-density foam such as good-quality upholstery foam is recommended. Foam comes in many shapes, so a visit to a specialist foam outlet will give you inspiration for new patterns.

You will need
piece of foam
hardboard, cut to the same size as the foam
wood glue or PVA (white) glue
felt-tipped pen
ruler
craft knife
small block of wood

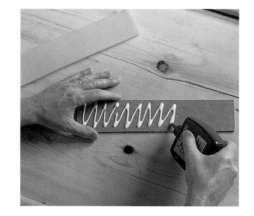

1 Stick the foam on to the hardboard by applying wood glue or PVA (white) glue to the rough side. Without waiting for the glue to set, draw the pattern on to the foam using a felt-tipped pen and ruler.

2 Use a craft knife to define the outline of the sections to be cut. Using wood glue or PVA glue, stick the wooden block in the middle of the stamp back, to act as a handle. Leave to dry thoroughly.

Linoleum

Cutting lino is a simple technique using special lino-cutting tools. You will be delighted with the intricacy of the motifs you can create.

You will need
tracing paper and pencil
lino block
sheet of transfer paper
masking tape
sharp pencil
craft knife
lino-cutting tools – a "U"-shaped scoop and a "V"-shaped gouge

1 Make a tracing of your chosen motif, the same size as the lino block. Slip a sheet of transfer paper (chalky side down) between the tracing and the lino, then tape the edges with masking tape. Draw over the pattern lines with a sharp pencil. The tracing will appear on the lino block.

2 Remove the transfer paper and cut around the outline with a craft knife. Cut any fine detail or straight lines by making shallow, angular cuts from each side, then scoop out the "V"-shaped sections.

3 Cut the rest of the pattern using the lino tools – the scoop for removing large areas of background, and the gouge for cutting finer curves and details. Hold the lino down firmly.

Different print effects

The images shown below were made by printing directly on to fabric, using different techniques and one or more colours. Experiment with the various fabrics, inks and paints available.

This print was made with a potato.

This print was made with a sponge.

This print was made with a stamp.

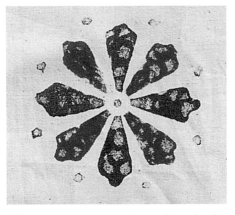

This print was made with a high-density foam stamp in two colours.

These prints were made using wine bottle corks bored with holes.

This print was made with a high-density foam stamp in a single colour.

This crisp fleur-de-lis print was made with a high-density foam stamp printed in one bold colour.

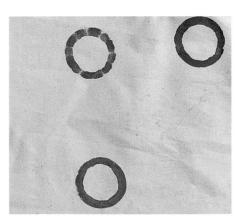

These circles were made using potato cuts, inked with two different colours to create an irregular pattern.

Designing with stamps

Explore the full potential of the thousands of ready-made stamps now available, by using them in interesting and unusual ways to give individual style to your hand-printed fabrics.

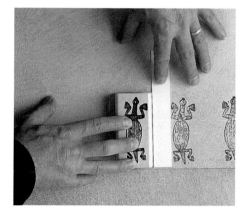

Rows

To create neat, regular rows, good spacing is vital. Decide on the space you want between prints and cut a strip of paper to that width. Use another paper strip to measure the distance between rows. Each time you make a print, place the strip against the edge and line up the edge of the printing block with the other side of the strip. Check right angles and corners with a set square (t-square).

Zigzags

Positioning a stamp at an angle will give a design extra interest. Make a print, then flip the shape over and repeat. Align the shape with the bottom edge of the fabric, or a line marked with tailor's chalk and a ruler.

Making large motifs

Stamps are usually quite small, but you can create a larger design by repeating a stamp, for example in the formation shown here. Use cut-out paper prints and experiment by placing them in spirals, circles and triangles, to create quite different effects.

Paper cut-outs

To help you visualize how a repeat pattern will look, make several prints on paper. Cut out the shapes and arrange them until you are satisfied, securing them with small pieces of masking tape if necessary.

Irregular patterns

If your design doesn't fit into a regular grid, plan the pattern on paper first. Cut out shapes to represent the spaces and use these to position the finished pattern.

Making a stencil

A wide range of stencil designs is available from craft suppliers, but it is very easy to make your own. Fabric paints used for stencilling should have a creamy consistency.

you will need

paper and pencil
tracing paper (optional)
felt-tipped pen
stencil card (card stock), Mylar film or
stencil acetate
craft knife and cutting mat
spray adhesive (stencil mount)
fabric paints
stencil brush or small sponge
iron

1 Draw your design freehand on paper or trace one of the templates at the back of the book. Using a felt-tipped pen, trace the design on to stencil card (card stock), Mylar film or stencil acetate.

2 Cut out the design using a craft knife and working on a cutting mat. It may be necessary to cut more than one stencil for the design to build up patterns and colours.

3 Apply spray adhesive (stencil mount) to the back of the stencil to hold it in place on the fabric.

4 Remove excess paint from the stencil brush or sponge by dabbing on to paper or spare fabric. Hold the stencil brush vertically and dab on paint gradually to build up colour. With a sponge, use a light painting movement. Apply the paint sparingly.

5 Carefully remove the stencil and leave the paint to dry. Fix (set) the fabric paint according to the manufacturer's instructions. Repeat step 3, placing the second stencil on top of the painted area. Repeat step 4, remove the stencil and leave to dry.

Special effects Stencilling is not difficult to master, but it is worth practising on a small area to get used to handling the brush and to become accustomed to the properties of the paints you are using.

This pattern was made by stippling (or dabbing) with a dry brush.

Use a dry brush with a tiny amount of paint and rotate the brush in circles.

This look was achieved by rotating and shading paint in two colours.

This rougher look was achieved by stippling the surface lightly.

Stipple the first colour, then add the second by working out from the centre

Apply each colour working from the sides into the centre.

Fill or block in the leaves with dense colour. Create the petals by rotating the brush over the stencil.

Work inwards from the edges so that the outer edges of the petals and leaves contain the most paint.

Apply the light shade first over the whole surface. Apply the second shade to just one side.

A simple grid of horizontal lines, drawn with a pencil and ruler, makes a very effective base for a stylishly modern pattern. Print it in varying tones of three different colours to give the design plenty of interest.

Block-printed Chair Pad

you will need

cotton-covered chair pad

strong scissors

felt-tipped pen

cardboard

newspaper

pencil

ruler

polystyrene (styrofoam) tray

piece of wool blanket

plastic spoon

plastic gloves

fabric printing inks in yellow, green and blue

small block of 2cm/¾in wood

fine artist's paintbrush

iron

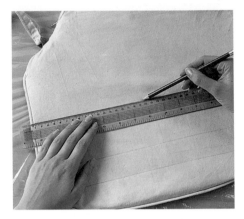

1 Remove the pad from the cushion cover. Cut a piece of cardboard to fit snugly inside the cover. Draw around the cardboard on a folded newspaper and cut this out about 5mm/¼in smaller than the cardboard. Cut about two newspapers for each side of the cushion. Slide half the sheets into the cover on top of the cardboard.

2 With a pencil and ruler, draw very light horizontal lines across the cover as a guide for printing. Space the lines a ruler's width apart. The lines could be drawn diagonally depending on the effect you wish to achieve.

3 Make a printing pad by lining a polystyrene (styrofoam) tray with a piece of blanket. Using a plastic spoon and wearing plastic gloves, put small amounts of the fabric printing inks on the pad. Replace the lids on the jars to stop the inks from drying out.

4 Practise printing first on a spare piece of fabric. Dip the block of wood into each of the inks, combining the colours on the block, then press down firmly on the fabric. You may get a second print from the block before reloading with ink.

5 Print the cushion cover, starting from the middle and working downwards in horizontal lines. Use the pencil guidelines to help you to keep the printed rows straight.

6 When the first half of one side is complete, turn the cover round to print the rest. Experiment with different printing blocks to achieve a range of designs.

7 Retouch the edges and any piping, using a fine paintbrush, combining the colours as before. Print on one side of the cushion ties. Leave to dry for 48 hours.

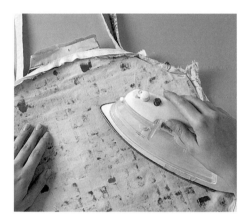

8 Empty the contents, and turn the cover inside out. Insert the cardboard. Press to fix (set) the inks. Remove the cardboard and turn right side out.

9 Turn the cover over, reinsert the cardboard and unused newspaper. Mark out the design lines on the second side. Print as before, finishing with the ties. Dry and fix, as before.

This plain pillowcase has an all-round border stamped with an floral design, and the top sheet folds back to reveal a matching border. Choose your own ready-made stamp and print in appropriate colours.

Stamped Bed Linen Borders

you will need
rubber stamp
scrap paper
scissors
cotton or polycotton sheet
and pillowcase
sheet of thin cardboard
fabric printing inks in dark green
and blue
scrap of spare fabric
iron

1 Stamp several motifs on scrap paper and cut them out. Arrange them along the sheet top edge or pillowcase border to work out the position and spacing of your pattern.

2 Place a sheet of cardboard under the fabric, to prevent the ink from soaking through. Apply dark green ink to parts of the stamp and blue ink to the other parts.

3 Test the colour by printing on a fabric scrap. When you are happy with the effect, lift the paper-stamped motifs one at a time, and stamp the bed linen in their place. Press firmly, giving the fabric time to absorb the ink. Print round the pillowcase and along the top of the sheet, adding ink to the stamp as it is needed. Press the wrong side with a warm, dry iron to set (fix) the inks.

Brighten up a child's playroom with these large cushions. Print the leaf motif in autumn colours, as here, or in two shades of green. Continue the theme with different stamped motifs on the walls and furniture.

Autumnal Floor Cushions

You will need

yellow cotton floor cushions

iron

paper scissors

large piece of cardboard

black stamp pad

leaf stamp

paper

fabric paints in ochre and dark brown

plate

small foam paint roller

1 Wash, dry and press the cushion covers. Cut a piece of cardboard to fit inside the first cushion cover. This will stop the paint from seeping through to the other side.

2 Using the black stamp pad, stamp a number of leaves on to scrap paper. Roughly cut out the paper leaves and arrange them in circles, as desired, on the cushion cover to plan your design.

3 Spread some ochre fabric paint on a plate. Thoroughly coat the foam roller with the paint, rolling it backwards and forwards. Print three alternate leaves, following the design.

4 Ink the stamp with dark brown paint in the same way, then fill in the spaces between the ochre leaves. Use the roller to re-ink the stamp as you work, to maintain the dark colour. Try not to overprint the ochre leaves. Allow the paint to dry thoroughly for several hours. Fix (set) the paints by pressing the wrong side of the fabric with a warm, dry iron, following the manufacturer's instructions.

Calico makes an ideal surface for fabric printing. Choose ready-made stamps for the borders and corners of the blind, then fill in the centre with a few extra motifs. Plan the design before you start.

Stamped Calico Blind

you will need

medium-weight calico

iron

tape measure

scissors

dressmaker's pins

fabric paints in different colours

plate

applicator sponges

high-density foam stamps

sewing machine

matching sewing thread

needle

pencil

1.5cm/⅝in brass eyelets and eyelet kit

nylon cord

2 spring toggles

9mm/⅜in wooden dowel cut to fit the width of the window frame

2 screw-in hooks

1 Wash, dry and press the calico. Measure the window. Cut two pieces of calico, 4cm/1½in wider than the window and 7cm/2¾in longer. This allows for hems and space for the eyelets. Set one piece aside for the lining.

2 On the other piece, use pins to mark out the area for the stamped design, 7cm/2¾in from each side, 5cm/2in from the top and 11cm/4½in from the bottom. If you wish, lightly mark the lines with a soft pencil. Spread out the fabric on a flat surface.

3 Squeeze out a small amount of each fabric paint on to a plate. Using an applicator sponge, apply an even coating of paint to each stamp.

4 Stamp your design on to the marked-out piece of calico, applying an even pressure. Apply fresh paint for each motif to keep the colour consistent. Allow the paints to dry between each colour application so that they do not smudge.

5 Complete the design and leave the paint to dry. Following the manufacturer's instructions, iron the calico on the wrong side to fix (set) the paints. Press under the hem allowance, 2cm/¾in at each side and the top, and 5cm/2in at the bottom. Open out the folds. With right sides together, pin the stamped calico to the plain piece of calico around all the edges.

6 Stitch using a 2cm/¾in seam at the top and sides and 5cm/2in at the bottom. Leave a gap for turning on one side and a gap at the top of each side seam for threading the dowel through.

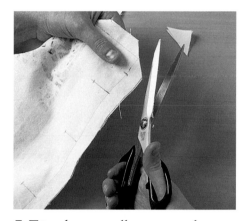

7 Trim the seam allowance at the corners. Turn the blind right side out, then press flat all the edges. Slip stitch the gap in the side seam by hand.

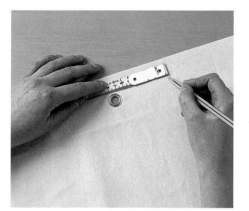

8 Mark the eyelet positions up each side edge of the blind about 7.5cm/3in apart. Carefully insert the eyelets using a kit and following the manufacturer's instructions.

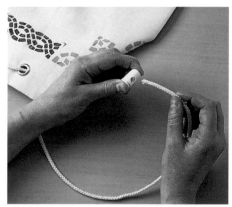

9 Thread a length of nylon cord through the eyelets, knotting it at the top. Thread each bottom end through a spring toggle. Knot each cord at the bottom and trim off the excess.

10 Thread the dowel through the gaps in the top corners of the blind. Screw two hooks into the top corners of the window frame from which to hang the reefer blind.

The humble potato is one of the best printing tools and is inexpensive. A cut potato exudes a starchy liquid that blends into the ink and adds translucence. Print a set of napkins to match your new tablecloth.

Potato-printed Tablecloth

you will need

old blanket

drawing (push) pins

white 100% cotton fabric, pre-washed and ironed, to fit your table

medium-size fresh potato

sharp kitchen knife

cutting board and craft knife

small artist's paintbrush

paper

leaf green water-based fabric printing ink (or use standard primary colours: yellow, blue and red)

sheet of glass (optional)

palette knife (optional)

small gloss paint roller

needle or sewing machine and matching sewing thread

iron

1 Pin the blanket to the work surface, using drawing (push) pins. Arrange the cotton tablecloth on top. Cut through the potato on a cutting board in one smooth movement to give a flat surface.

2 Practise painting the clover leaf on paper, drawing the shape freehand. When you are confident, paint the shape on the potato using ink.

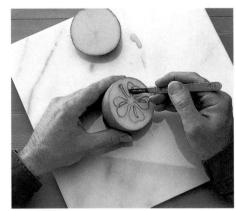

3 Using the craft knife, cut around the outline, cutting away the waste potato to a depth of about 5mm/¼in.

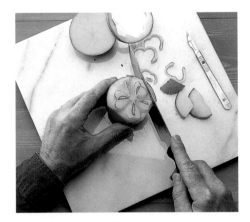

4 Using a kitchen knife, trim the potato into a square. Then cut a groove all around, about halfway down, to make it easier to hold.

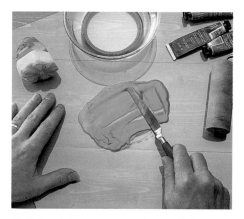

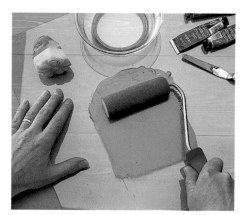

5 If you are using primary colours, mix green from yellow and blue. Then mix two parts green ink with one part blue and one-quarter part red.

6 Blend the colours thoroughly on a sheet of glass to achieve a consistent colour, using a palette knife.

7 Run the small paint roller through the ink until it is thoroughly coated.

8 Apply an even coating of ink to the surface of the potato stamp.

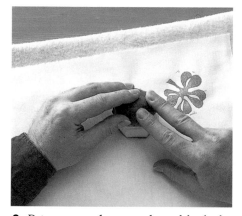

9 Print at random on the tablecloth. Re-ink the potato after every two prints to vary the intensity of the colour. Leave to dry, then fix (set) the paints using a warm dry iron, following the manufacturer's instructions. Hem the raw edges of the tablecloth by hand or machine.

Transform a canvas chair with the simple technique of sponge printing. The sponged diamonds are outlined with a bold "running stitch" stencil. Choose a chair in which the back and seat are easily removable.

Diamond-printed Director's Chair

you will need
red director's chair
nylon massage puff or soft sponge
fabric paints in pink, orange and blue
paint-mixing container
ruler
tailor's chalk
felt-tipped pen
sponge pan-cleaner with
scouring surface
scissors (optional)
craft knife
Mylar film

1 Remove the canvas seat and back from the chair. Using a nylon massage puff or a soft sponge, apply pink fabric paint to the fabric to break up the solidity of the background colour. Leave to dry.

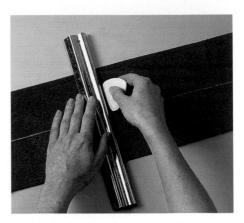

2 Using a ruler, determine the centre of the seat and back pieces and mark with tailor's chalk.

3 With a felt-tipped pen, draw a horizontal and a vertical line across the sponge pan-cleaner to divide it into four equal sections. Next draw through the mid-points on each side to make a diamond shape.

4 Cut the corners off the sponge pan-cleaner using scissors or a craft knife, to make the diamond shape. Dab the sponge pan-cleaner into orange paint, scourer side down, so that it is evenly covered with paint.

5 Print the first row of diamonds along the centre line of each fabric piece. Match the horizontal lines on the sponge pan-cleaner with the chalked lines on the fabric to ensure that you print in a straight line.

6 Continue to print orange diamonds across the fabric, aligning the points carefully, until the entire surface of the canvas has been decorated.

7 Using a felt-tipped pen, mark a "running stitch" line on a piece of Mylar film. Cut it out with a craft knife. Place the stencil over the design and use a piece of sponge to dab on blue paint. Remove the stencil, wipe away the excess paint, and repeat in the other diagonal direction, using blue or orange paint.

Feathers make wonderfully delicate prints, especially on a floating, see-through fabric such as muslin (cheesecloth). Here the top of the curtain has been finished with a wide border and ties in a darker shade.

Feather-printed Curtain

you will need

muslin (cheesecloth) fabric, to fit your window

iron

protective paper or cloth

fine artist's paintbrush

fabric paints in two complementary colours

large feathers (e.g. pheasant)

paper

maribou feather trim (optional)

needle and matching sewing thread (optional)

1 Press the muslin (cheesecloth) with a hot iron. Cover your work surface with a protective layer of paper or cloth, and arrange the muslin flat. Using a fine paintbrush, coat a feather with one of the fabric paints.

2 Ensure the feather is not too thickly coated so that the fine hairs will print clearly. Position the painted feather carefully on the fabric.

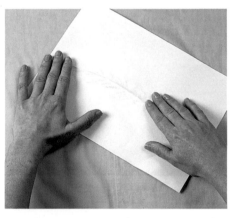

3 Place a piece of paper over the feather and rub gently over the top with the palm of your hand. Remove and discard the paper.

4 With clean hands, carefully remove the feather to reveal a print on the fabric surface.

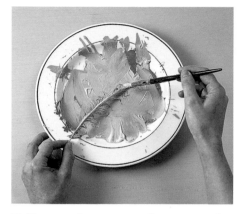

5 For an alternative effect, paint the next feather with a lighter shade of the same colour of paint.

6 Position the second feather partly over the base of the previously printed feather. Place a piece of paper over it and rub gently as before. Carefully remove the paper and the feather to reveal a print with a three-dimensional shadow effect.

7 If desired, for a fun treatment, decorate the hem of the curtain by sewing on a length of maribou trim by hand.

Use real leaves to print this linen table runner in rich autumnal tones. Choose an interesting selection of different-shaped leaves, large and small. The finished size is 45 x 130cm/18 x 51in.

Leaf-printed Table Runner

you will need

iron

off-white herringbone-weave linen, trimmed to 50 x 135cm/20 x 53in

ruler

scissors

sewing machine and sewing thread

newspaper

mixed sizes and types of leaves (e.g. geranium, birch, oak)

fabric paints in terracotta, mustard and burnt umber

A4 (210 x 297mm/8¼ x 11½in) sheet of plastic or polypropylene

fabric medium

7.5cm/3in-wide paint roller

paper

small rolling pin

sponge

1 Press under a 1cm/½in hem all around the linen. Open out. Measure and mark 3cm/1¼in from each corner on the edges. Cut off the corners. With right sides together, fold the fabric diagonally so that raw edges align. Stitch the cut corners to form a mitre. Repeat. Turn the corners out and press. Stitch a 1cm/½in hem. Press.

2 Arrange the leaves in the desired pattern. Cover the work surface with newspaper and spread out the fabric, right side up on top. Arrange the leaves on the table runner in the desired pattern. Begin printing the leaves at the other end of the runner so that you can follow the pattern that you have made.

3 Pour a small amount of each colour on to separate areas of the sheet of plastic, followed by a small amount of fabric medium on top of each. Roll the roller backwards and forwards through the first colour to mix in the fabric medium and to cover the roller.

4 Place the first leaf on a piece of scrap paper, top side down – the veins are more prominent on the back of the leaves. Hold the leaf by its stem and roll the paint-covered roller over the back of the leaf until it is covered with paint.

5 Position the paint-covered leaf on the table runner in the desired position. Firmly roll over it once with a small, clean rolling pin. Wipe the rolling pin clean with a damp sponge immediately after use, then rinse out the sponge. Remove the leaf carefully from the fabric with clean hands.

6 Each leaf can be used a few times, and it is not necessary to clean the leaves between colours, as the subtle blending of shades will enhance the overall effect. Continue building up the pattern, changing leaves and colours as desired. Remember that the paint of the previous leaf print will still be wet.

7 When the table runner is completely covered with the printed leaf pattern, leave to dry for several hours. Using a warm dry iron, press the wrong side of the table runner to fix (set) the paints, following the manufacturer's instructions.

Many fruits and vegetables make excellent stamps. Here an apple and a pear are used to print the border of a blind and a matching set of calico curtains for a co-ordinated window treatment.

Fruit-printed Blind and Curtains

you will need

scissors

tape measure

unbleached muslin (cheesecloth)

unbleached calico

iron

dressmaker's pins

sewing machine

matching sewing thread

tacking (basting) thread

needle

tailor's chalk

transparent net tape

kitchen knife

apple and pear

fabric paints in red, green and black

medium artist's paintbrush

thick cardboard

small plastic rings

9mm/⅜in wooden dowel lengths cut to the width of the finished blind

nylon cord

staple gun

wooden batten, to fit your window recess

2 screw-eyes

cleat

pencil-pleat curtain tape

1 To make the blind, cut the muslin (cheesecloth) 4cm/1½in wider and 7cm/2¾in longer than the window. For the border, cut strips of calico 13cm/5in wide, and 13cm/5in longer than the side edges and 25cm/10in longer than the bottom edge of the muslin. Mitre the bottom corners of the border strips, by cutting the lower ends of the side strips and both ends of the bottom strip at a 45° angle.

2 Press a 2cm/¾in hem to the wrong side along the inside edge of each border. Pin and stitch the mitres together, then press the seams flat. Pin and stitch the right side of the border to the wrong side of the muslin, using a 2cm/¾in seam. Trim the seam and clip each corner. Turn the border through to the right side and press. Pin, tack (baste) and machine top stitch the border piece close to the fold.

3 Divide the blind into horizontal sections no more than 30cm/12in deep, making the bottom section shorter. On the wrong side, stitch transparent net tape along each line.

4 Cut the apple and the pear in half. Using a paintbrush, apply red paint to the apple and green to the pear. Print around the calico border. Re-coat the fruits with paint after each print.

5 Cut a small piece of cardboard and bend it slightly. Dip the thin edge into a little black fabric paint and print a stalk on each fruit. Leave to dry.

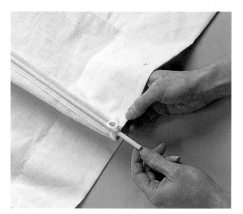

6 Turn the blind over and stitch a small plastic ring to each end of the net tape channels, then insert a length of dowel in each channel.

7 Tie a length of nylon cord to each ring of the lowest channel, then thread it through the other rings to the top. Use a staple gun to attach the blind to the top of the batten. Place a screw-eye in the bottom of the batten over each line of rings and thread the cords through, taking both cords to one side of the blind. Twist the cords and wrap them around a cleat positioned towards the lower half of the window recess or frame.

8 For the curtains, cut the calico to the length required plus 12.5cm/5in. Press and stitch a double 2.5cm/1in hem down each side, and a double 5cm/2in hem along the lower edge. Press under a 2.5cm/1in hem at the top. Cut the curtain tape 5cm/2½in longer than the curtain width.

9 Draw out the cords from one end of the curtain tape and knot the ends. Fold under the knotted end of the tape and pin it to the curtain 5mm/¼in from the upper edge. Tuck in the raw edges of the tape at the other end. Stitch in place along the guidelines without catching in the cords. Using the apple and pear halves as before, print a random design all over the curtains. Add the stalks with cardboard.

Fresh yellow gingham borders make an attractive background for this horse and foal, printed with foam rubber sponge. The squares on the gingham will help you to space and position the motifs accurately.

Sponge-printed Gingham Bed Linen

you will need

tracing paper and pen

spray adhesive (stencil mount)

24 x 24cm/9½ x 9½in thick cardboard

scissors

24 x 24 x 1cm/9½ x 9½ x ½in high-density foam rubber

ballpoint pen

iron

2.1m/7ft of 90cm/36in-wide yellow gingham fabric

tablespoon

base medium

fabric paints in red, ultramarine blue, jade green and white

2cm/¾in decorator's paintbrush

fine and medium artist's paintbrushes

flat white single-size bed sheet

dressmaker's pins

sewing machine

white sewing thread

white pillowcase

1 Trace the two horses from the back of the book. Using spray adhesive, mount the tracing paper on to a piece of cardboard. Leave the adhesive to dry, then cut out the horses.

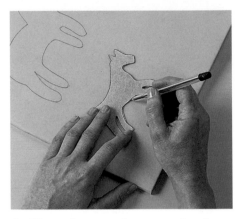

2 Place the templates on the foam rubber, trace around them with a ballpoint pen and cut out. Iron the fabric. Cut strips of fabric the sheet width by 21cm/8½in deep plus 3cm/1¼in seam allowances. For the pillowcase, cut a strip 21cm/8½in deep by the pillow width, plus seam allowances.

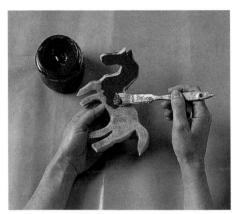

3 Add a loaded tablespoon of base medium to each pot of red, blue and green paint. For light blue, mix white paint into the ultramarine. Using the decorator's paintbrush, apply red paint to one side of a foam horse. The foam will absorb some of the paint; so dab it on until the paint sits on the surface.

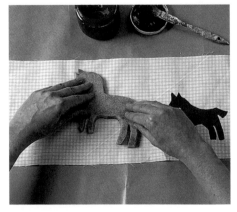

4 Test the print on a fabric scrap. Place the back hoof 3cm/1¼in from the bottom edge, with the front of the horse prancing up. Press the foam firmly. Lift the foam. Print the sheet strip, working across from one end, and alternating the horse and the foal. Leave to dry.

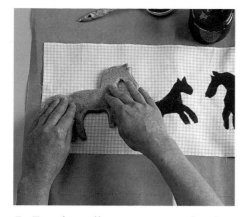

5 For the pillowcase, print the first horse and foal, then wash the sponge thoroughly, squeeze out all the water and allow the sponge to dry. Apply red paint to the other side of the sponge in the same way and print so that the last horse faces the horse and foal. Leave to dry.

6 Using jade green paint and a fine artist's paintbrush, add tufts of grass in short strokes between each horse. Leave to dry. Using light blue, paint the hooves and manes, and add a stripe of colour to the tops of the tails. Leave to dry for several hours. Fix (set) the paints following the manufacturer's instructions, pressing on the wrong side with a warm, dry iron.

7 Press under a 1.5cm/⅝in hem at the bottom edge and sides of the printed sheet strip, and around the pillowcase slip. Pin the sheet strip with the printed side facing the wrong side of the bed sheet, and pin the edges together. Stitch 1.5cm/⅝in from the edge. Press the seam open. Flip the printed gingham edge over and press flat.

8 Pin the bottom and sides of the gingham into position on the top of the sheet. Top stitch the printed gingham along the top, bottom and sides of the sheet. Press under a 1.5cm/⅝in seam allowance around the pillowcase. Place the gingham strip for the pillowcase on the open edge, face up. Pin all around the edges, matching the hems with the existing hems and seams. Top stitch, keeping the stitching close to the hemmed edges so that it does not interfere with placing the pillow into the casing.

Decorate a tie-on seat pad with stylized leaf motifs. Trace the motifs on to linoleum and mount them on small wooden blocks. Print the leaves at random or plan out a design using tailor's chalk.

Lino-printed Leaves

you will need

soft pencil and paper

tracing paper

linoleum

linoleum cutting tool

wooden blocks

handsaw

hammer and nails (optional)

strong adhesive

scissors

wild silk fabric, pre-washed

tape measure

iron

masking tape

absorbent cloth

dressmaker's pins

opaque iron-fix (-set) fabric paints in 3 colours

paint palette or separate plates

medium artist's paintbrushes

ribbon

sewing machine

matching sewing thread

wadding (batting) cut to size

needle

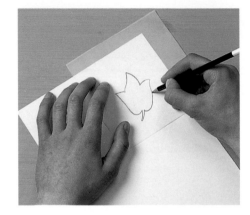

1 Trace the leaf shapes provided on to a piece of paper. Trace them and transfer to the linoleum, one motif per lino piece. To do this, rub over the back of the tracing paper with a soft pencil, place the tracing right side up on the lino and re-trace over the drawn lines. If the lines appear faint, go over them with a pencil.

2 Use a linoleum cutting tool to cut away the areas that you don't want to print. Cut a wooden block to fit the design. If you like, nail a smaller cube to the back to act as a handle. Using a strong adhesive, glue the lino design to the flat side of the wood block. Make up several blocks with different designs in this way.

3 Cut two squares of silk to fit the chair seat, plus a 2.5cm/1in seam allowance all round. Wash one square and iron flat while still damp. Tape an absorbent cloth to the work surface, then pin the silk square to it.

4 Mix up the paints. Using a paintbrush, coat the first block with paint and press it firmly on to the silk. Repeat, using different blocks and colours, then leave to dry. Remove the silk. Fix (set) the paints, following the manufacturer's instructions.

5 Pin the back and front right sides together. Inside the back edge place four ribbon ties. Stitch around the edge leaving a gap. Turn right side out. Place the wadding (batting) inside the cover, fold in the seam allowance and pin. Hand stitch the open side.

Print a jaunty sailing boat on to cotton fabric, decorate it with simple embroidery stitches, then appliqué it on to a hand towel as a novel decoration for your bathroom.

Foam-printed Boat Towel

you will need

high-density sponge, e.g.
upholstery foam (foam rubber)
craft knife and cutting mat
metal ruler
stiff cardboard
PVA (white) glue
paper
scissors
felt-tipped pen
plain light-coloured cotton fabric
masking tape
fabric paints
plate or palette
paintbrush
embroidery hoop
stranded embroidery thread (floss)
embroidery needle
dressmaker's pins
hand towel
8 pearl buttons

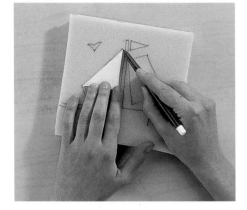

1 Cut a 15cm/6in square and a 15 x 5cm/6 x 2in rectangle of sponge to make the stamps. Cut a piece of cardboard for each piece and glue one on to each sponge. Scale up the designs at the back of the book as required. Make paper templates and cut them out. Draw around the boat and wave designs on the square sponge, using a felt-tipped pen.

2 Carefully cut away the excess sponge using a craft knife and metal ruler. Repeat on the rectangular sponge, positioning the waves so that they will fall between the first set. Cut a 17cm/7in square of cotton and tape it to the work surface, pulling the fabric taut.

◀ **3** Load the boat stamp with paint. Centre the stamp over the fabric and press. Remove the stamp. Leave to dry. Load the waves stamp with paint and stamp another set of waves between the first set. Re-load the wave stamp with paint and position it 1cm/½in from the bottom edge. Apply the stamp, aligning it with the bottom edge. Print the birds at a 45° angle above the waves. Stamp on to the fabric and leave to dry.

4 Fix (set) the paints by pressing on the wrong side with a warm, dry iron. Insert the panel in an embroidery hoop and work running stitch in stranded embroidery thread (floss) to pick out the clouds and details on the sails and boat.

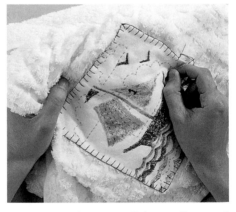

5 Press under a small hem all round and centre at one end of the towel. Blanket stitch the panel in place.

6 Stitch a pearl button to each corner of the panel, and one in the middle of each side.

These bold lino-printed motifs, stamped in pale ink on a dark-coloured fabric, create a very striking effect. Interlaced satin ribbons divide the design into a grid.

Mexican Motif Place Mats

you will need

ruler

scissors

1.2m/4ft plain-weave cotton

bodkin

tracing paper and pencil

linoleum

linoleum-cutting tools

carbon paper

medium artist's paintbrush

cream fabric paint

paper

18m/19½yd of 1cm/½in-wide satin ribbon in two colours

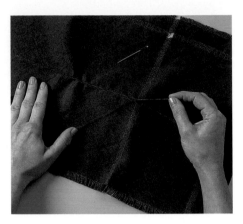

1 Cut the fabric along the weave into six rectangles, each 50 x 35cm/20 x 14in. Pull out the threads along all four edges of each mat to make a fringe about 1.5cm/⅝in deep. Using a bodkin and scissors, draw out a 1.5cm/⅝in-wide section of vertical threads 2.5cm/1in from each short side, and two sections each 6.5cm/2½in from the vertical centre.

2 Following the same measurements, draw out three sections of horizontal threads from the mat at the top, centre and bottom. At the point where the lines of withdrawn threads cross will be a complete square. Trace the motif at the back of the book. Cut linoleum to the size of the motif and, using carbon paper and a pencil, transfer the motif on to the lino.

3 Using a fine V-shaped lino-cutting tool, carefully cut along the outline of the motif. Using a broader U-shaped blade, gouge out the excess lino. Make a few test prints with paint on some scrap paper. Using a paintbrush, apply just a small amount of fabric paint to the raised motif. Firmly press the loaded stamp on the mat and apply even pressure.

4 Remove the stamp and repeat until the pattern is complete. Leave the paint to dry. Using a bodkin, thread lengths of satin ribbon through the drawn-thread sections. Tidy the ends of the ribbons.

Traditional Indian textile printing blocks are widely available in many delicate patterns. The measurements quoted here can be adapted to suit your own design.

Block-printed Velvet Cushion

you will need

tape measure and dressmaker's pins
1.5m/1½yd of 90cm/36in-wide velvet
scissors
sewing machine and sewing thread
4 gold tassels
bronze powder
fabric-painting medium
plate or palette
medium decorator's paintbrush
thin cardboard
Indian textile-printing border block
iron and towel
3 gold buttons
needle
56cm/22in cushion pad

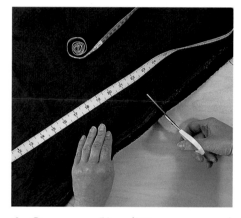

1 Cut out a 58cm/23in square and two rectangles 33 x 58cm/13 x 23in from velvet. To make the back of the cushion, turn under, pin and machine stitch a double hem along one long edge of each rectangle. Make three buttonholes, evenly spaced, in one long hem of one rectangle.

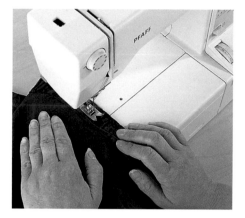

2 With right sides together, pin the buttonholed piece to the square front on three sides. Pin the other rectangle, stitched hems overlapping on top. Insert a tassel in the seam at each corner, facing in. Stitch and turn the cover through. Flatten the seams and place the cover on a flat surface.

3 Add one part bronze powder to two parts fabric-painting medium. Mix thoroughly. Insert a piece of cardboard inside the cushion. Paint an even coat of the mixture on to the block, position it along one edge of the cover and press down firmly. Repeat to complete the border design.

4 When the paint is dry, remove the cardboard. Fix (set) the paint, using a warm, dry iron following the manufacturer's instructions (rest the fabric on a towel). Hand stitch a gold button opposite each buttonhole on the back of the cover. Insert the cushion pad and fasten the buttons to finish.

A combination of stencilling and sponging is used to print this ready-made duvet cover. The light-coloured sponging creates a loose, painterly effect, while the stencils look precise and sharp-edged.

Summery Duvet Cover

you will need

absorbent cloth

pale-coloured, ready-made cotton
duvet cover, pre-washed

seam ripper

dressmaker's pins

iron

tracing paper and pencil

Mylar film or stencil card (card stock)

marker pen

craft knife and cutting mat

tailor's chalk

string

fabric paints in various light colours

plates

household sponge

spray adhesive (stencil mount)

small sponges or stencil brushes

sewing machine

matching sewing thread

1 Cover the work surface with an absorbent cloth. Carefully unpick the sides of the duvet cover and open it out into a large rectangle. Roll up the underside of the cover and pin it so that it is out of the way. Iron flat the upper side of the duvet area to be painted.

2 Enlarge the templates at the back of the book to the required size. Transfer on to Mylar film or stencil card (card stock) using a marker pen. On a cutting mat, accurately cut out the stencils with a craft knife.

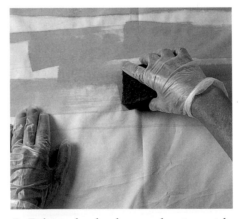

4 Dilute the background paint with water to the consistency of ink. Using a sponge, fill in the stripes. When each section of paint is dry, move on to the next; do not move the fabric while it is wet as this may cause smudging. When the duvet is painted, leave it to dry. Fix (set) the paints with a warm, dry iron following the manufacturer's instructions.

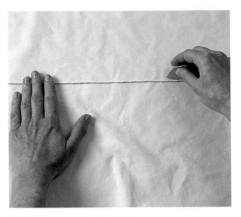

3 Using tailor's chalk, mark stripes at the duvet edge, deep enough for the stencils to fit inside. Mark the midpoint on each stripe. Stretch and pin a piece of string across the duvet from side to side. Rule across these lines.

5 Coat the reverse of one of the stencils with spray adhesive (stencil mount). Place it on the midpoint of a stripe and apply contrasting colours, using a small sponge or stencil brush. Carefully remove the stencil.

 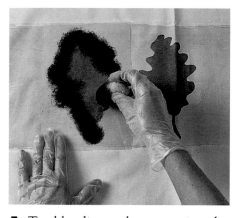 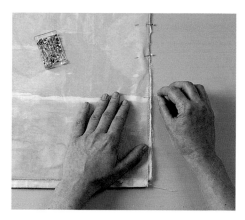

6 Continue along the stripes adding motifs, keeping them evenly spaced. After removing the stencil from the fabric, wipe away the excess paint to keep the colours clear and prevent paint from seeping on to the fabric.

7 Try blending colours to give the motifs a textured look. When your stencilling is complete and the paint is dry, fix (set) the paints according to the manufacturer's instructions, by pressing the wrong side with an iron.

8 Pin, then machine stitch the side seams to remake the duvet cover. The fabric may be stiff, but washing the duvet cover should ease this; follow the paint manufacturer's instructions for washing temperatures.

This stunning single-bed quilt was inspired by an appliqué quilt made around 1840. The design is called Willow Oak. Spray paint is quicker to work with, but you can use ordinary fabric paint if you prefer.

Stencilled Quilt

you will need

tracing paper and pencil

stencil card (card stock)

craft knife and cutting mat

2 single cotton sheets, dipped in tea, dried and ironed

2 long straight edges or rulers

masking tape

set square (t-square)

brown paper

spray adhesive (stencil mount)

navy or black spray fabric paint

iron

tailor's chalk

scissors

wadding (batting) to fit the quilt size, plus a little extra all round

dressmaker's pins

needle

tacking (basting) thread

sewing machine

cream sewing thread

1 Enlarge the templates from the back of the book and cut out of stencil card (card stock). Fold the sheet in quarters, crease the folds, then unfold. Place the grid stencil along the centre fold. Mask off the fabric all around to protect it from drifting spray. Stick the back of the stencil with spray adhesive (stencil mount) firmly on the fabric. Spray the stencil with paint, then work in blocks above and below the centre line to complete the grid.

2 Stencil a large motif inside each square. Add the corner motifs, then the border motifs. Allow to dry.

3 Press the stencilled quilt top. With the right side uppermost, using tailor's chalk, draw a line all round the design then mark a second line 3cm/1¼in outside the first line. Trim the excess fabric around the edge of the design, leaving an extra 5cm/2in all round.

4 Cut a piece of wadding (batting) the same size as the printed quilt top. Cut the plain sheet larger. Arrange it right side down. Centre the wadding on top, then the printed sheet, right side up. Starting in the centre, pin, then tack (baste) the layers together.

◄ **5** Place a strip of masking tape diagonally across the centre of the quilt, then a second, about 10cm/4in away. Use the strips as a quilting guide. Emphasize the motifs by working running stitch around each through all the layers. Alternatively, roll the quilt diagonally, so that it will fit under a sewing machine. Machine quilt the grid, then the perimeter line. Finish off the thread ends on the back by tying and trimming them.

6 On the back, mark a line 3cm/1¼in out from the perimeter stitching. Trim the wadding and backing to this line. Trim the quilt front 5cm/2in larger all around. Turn the excess fabric of the printed front over to the quilt back. Turn in a 1.5cm/½in hem all around the raw edges of the quilt front. Pin and slip stitch the folded edge in place, stitching through the backing only. Neatly mitre the corners on the back of the quilt.

Decorate a cotton tablecloth with a mosaic border, subtly printed in three shades of blue. The stencil will take time to cut, but the finished results are worth it. Fill in the centre of the cloth with extra star motifs.

Mosaic-stencilled Tablecloth

you will need

iron

cream-coloured cotton fabric, to fit your table

sewing machine and sewing thread

tracing paper and pencil

craft knife and cutting mat

Mylar film

masking tape

stencil brushes

fabric paints in dark blue, pale blue and light aqua

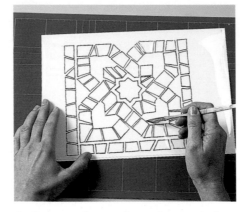

1 Press under and machine stitch a 2.5cm/1in-wide double hem around the fabric. Using tracing paper and a pencil, trace the template at the back of the book. Place the tracing on a cutting mat with a piece of Mylar film on top and secure with masking tape. Using a craft knife, cut out each piece of the pattern.

2 Position the traced stencil on one edge of the tablecloth and secure with small strips of tape. Using a stencil brush, take up a small amount of dark blue paint and carefully apply to the outer border of the stencil.

3 Apply pale blue paint to the inner sections of the design, leaving the central star motif clear.

4 Apply light aqua paint to the central star motif. Remove the stencil and place it in the next position along the edge of the tablecloth. Repeat until the border design is complete. Stencil the central star motif randomly over the tablecloth.

This elegant lampshade is first sponged with a white-and-gold base, then stencilled with a black motif. The gold highlights are a perfect finishing touch.

Elizabethan Pattern Lampshade

you will need

cotton lampshade

fabric paints in black, white and gold

small piece of sponge

tracing paper and pencil

Mylar film

craft knife and cutting mat

white paper

stencil brush

masking tape

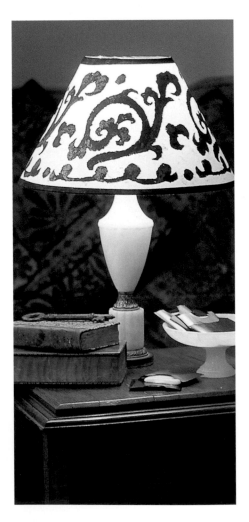

1 Apply the base colours of white and gold to the lampshade using a sponge. Take up only a small amount of fabric paint each time, so that the texture of the sponge is transferred to the shade. Leave to dry.

2 Enlarge the template at the back of the book to fit your lampshade and trace on to a sheet of Mylar film. Using a craft knife, cut out the design. Place it on white paper and, using a stencil brush, dab undiluted black fabric paint on to the cut-out areas to practice the technique.

3 With masking tape, attach the stencil to the shade. Using the stencil brush, apply small amounts of black paint, gradually building up the density of colour. Carefully remove the stencil and leave the paint to dry.

4 Move the stencil to the next position and apply paint until the whole shade is patterned. Leave to dry. Re-tape the stencil to the shade, placing it over the previous work. Using the sponge, apply gold highlights.

This lively design uses car-spray paints, blended together to give a watery effect. Work in a ventilated area and use woven shower curtain fabric. Wash the finished item with a sponge.

Fish-stencilled Shower Curtain

you will need

tracing paper and pencil

marker pen

Mylar film or stencil card (card stock)

craft knife and cutting mat

woven polyester cotton shower curtain

spray adhesive (stencil mount)

masking tape

paper

car-spray paints in various colours

protective face mask

sponge

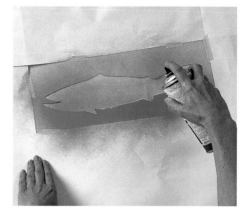

1 Enlarge the fish provided. Using a marker pen, trace the outlines on to Mylar film or stencil card (card stock). Cut out with a craft knife. On separate film, cut out the details within the outline. Do not cut away too much from the stencil or it will fall apart. If necessary, do a third and fourth stencil.

2 Protect the work surface then place the shower curtain flat, on top. Attach the fish stencil to the curtain using spray adhesive (stencil mount). Tape scrap paper around the stencil to protect the rest of the curtain. Using car-spray paints and wearing a protective face mask, start to fill in the cut-out areas of the stencil.

3 Subtle blends of colour can be achieved by using spray paints. Experiment first on a piece of scrap paper. Continue, positioning the fish randomly. When you are happy with the effect, spray the fish over the shower curtain.

4 For fish facing the opposite direction, cut new stencils: instead of re-drawing the design, stencil the fish on to the Mylar film or stencil card (card stock) with spray paint and cut out as before.

Fabric Painting

You do not need to be an expert artist or have trained drawing skills to paint beautiful designs and create your own unique fabrics. You can express your creativity by drawing simple, stylized shapes freehand, measuring out geometric patterns, or tracing the templates at the back of the book. Explore the exciting combinations of different colours and fabrics!

Dabbling with a Brush

Painting directly on to fabric differs from printing or stencilling because you are not confined to using a repeat image in the form of a block, stamp or stencil. Painting freehand means that each individual image will look spon-

taneous. Several of the projects included in this chapter are bold, colourful and fun to do, but at the other end of the spectrum you can also create delicate painted fabrics such as chiffon or organza.

There are a great many natural fabrics suitable for painting on – silk, cotton, wool and linen all accept fabric paints readily; man-made fabrics may not take up the colour with such intensity, but it is always worth experimenting. Fabric paints are available in various forms such as pens or with a nozzle-shaped applicator, which makes precise drawing of your design much

easier. These paints are specially designed for use on fabric, so the consistency will be correct and consistent. Thicken paint with the addition of various thickening agents, or dilute it with water to achieve a special effect such as a colourwashed background.

Follow the instructions given in the projects until you become familiar enough with the paints to begin to experiment.

For a large design such as a wall hanging or floorcloth, which will not need to be washed, it is

much less expensive to use ordinary household paints such as acrylic or emulsion (latex). Seal floorcloths with varnish to protect the finished design. Other painting media such as oil pastel sticks are ideal for small designs such as lampshades, which do not need regular washing.

Extra textural interest can be added to simple designs with stripes of ribbon or braid placed alongside flat painted stripes, or multi-coloured buttons that are practical as well as delightfully decorative. Embroidery stitches, worked by hand or sewing machine, can be used very effectively to add sophisticated or simple details to painted motifs, bringing a three-dimensional quality to the painted fabric surface and emphasizing or repeating the motifs and shapes.

Fabric paints are available in various forms from solid oil sticks and powders to felt-tipped pens, and are ideal for painting a range of designs and surfaces. Household paints are useful for larger projects.

Materials

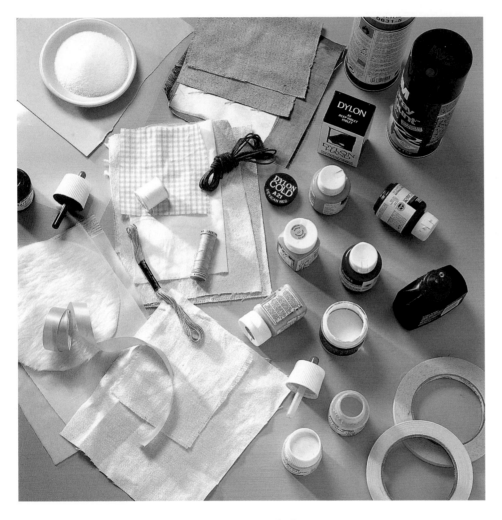

Acrylic paint
Use for large wall hangings or floorcloths that do not need to be washed.

Embroidery thread (floss)
Available in a wide range, so choose thread (floss) to suit the weight of fabric you are working with.

Emulsion (latex) paint
Use to paint floorcloths or wall hangings that will not need to be washed.

Fabrics
Natural fabrics provide the best surface for hand painting, and there is a wide variety to choose from. The fabrics used in this chapter include linen, velvet and cotton duck canvas as well as delicate fabrics such as chiffon and organza. Pre-wash washable fabrics.

Always protect the work surface. Insert thin cardboard inside cushion covers to prevent the paint from spreading through to the other side.

Fabric medium
Use to thicken fabric paint.

Fabric paints
The wide range of permanent fabric paints available includes metallic colours such as gold, bronze and silver. Many are fixed (set) by ironing with a warm dry iron, but always read the manufacturer's instructions. Paints are also available in pen form, which makes drawing designs very simple.

Gum thickener or anti-spread
Use to thicken fabric paint.

Oil pastel sticks
Use like crayons to draw on to surfaces that will not need to be washed. Available in a wide range of colours.

Powder pigments
Use to colour substances. Can be mixed with malt vinegar and sugar to make a traditional glaze.

Ribbons
Ribbons and braids are used to add textural interest. Attach with fabric glue or machine stitching.

Varnish
Use gloss, matt (flat) acrylic or polyurethane varnish to seal floorcloths. Use separate brushes to apply varnish.

Choose paintbrushes and other equipment to suit the size of your project, whether it be a large canvas floorcloth or a delicate chiffon scarf. Larger projects require larger equipment and work space.

Equipment

Masking tape/Carpet tape

Use to temporarily mask off areas of background fabric. Leave the paint to dry before removing the tape.

Needles

Choose a size of needle to suit the thread (floss) used. Use an ordinary needle for hand sewing.

Paintbrushes

Use a fine artist's paintbrush to paint a precise design, and to add details. Use larger paintbrushes for large items.

Pens and pencils

Use a soft pencil to trace templates and a sharp pencil or felt-tipped pen to draw lines with a straight edge.

Plate or palette

Use to hold paint and to mix various colours together.

Carbon transfer paper

Use to transfer designs on to fabric. Place the paper chalk-side down underneath a tracing. Using a large embroidery needle, prick through both layers of paper, making a close line of holes to transfer the design on to the fabric.

Craft knife

Use to cut cardboard. Use a sharp blade and work on a cutting mat.

Silk pins (Push pins)

Use to secure fabric when stretched taut on a wooden frame.

Dressmaker's pins

Use to temporarily hold pieces of fabric together.

Fabric glue

Use to attach ribbon and braid to projects that do not require washing. Use sparingly or the glue will mark.

Ruler/Straight edge/Tape measure

Use to mark out large designs.

Sponges

Small natural sponges give a mottled paint effect. Use a larger household sponge to cover large areas of fabric.

Vanishing fabric marker

Available in pen form. Use to trace or draw designs directly on to fabric.

Different painting tools will make a different mark on different types of fabric, and the consistency of the paint will also vary the effect. Experiment with new tools on paper before starting a project.

Techniques

Paint effects   A paintbrush is not a requisite to create different paint effects – use your fingers, sponges, rags, cotton wool buds (swabs) and toothbrushes.

Gently dab on paint with a small natural sponge to give a mottled effect. The amount of paint loaded on the sponge will vary the effect.

Use a larger household sponge to cover large areas of fabric with paint.

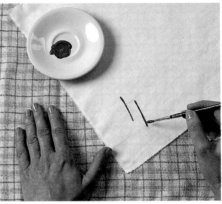

A fine artist's paintbrush is ideal for painting a precise design, as well as for adding details.

Paint applied to wet fabric will "bleed" slightly as it mixes with the water to make a soft, feathery edge.

Paint applied very sparingly with a large decorator's paintbrush makes light, open marks. Used vertically, then horizontally, it creates a cross-hatched effect.

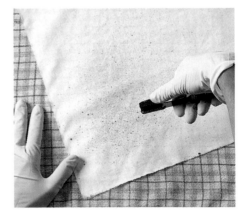

To create a light, speckled effect, dip a toothbrush in paint, shake off the excess, then flick the surface of the bristles with your thumb.

Colourwashing

This is a simple method of applying colour to a background. Wonderful effects can be achieved as colours merge together.

1 Wash the fabric to remove any dressing. Watered-down paint can be applied directly on to damp fabric with a brush. The effect will be random as moisture helps the paint to spread and diffuse over the fabric surface. This method will dilute the paint colour. Alternatively, apply several colours of paint to dry fabric without waiting for the first to dry. The colours will blend into each other on the fabric surface.

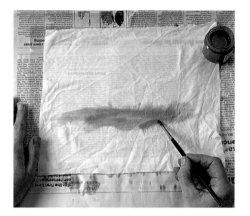

2 Use a brush in proportion with the design you are creating. Load with paint and apply to the fabric.

3 Apply the next colour by painting directly over the edge of the previous colour, to allow the colours to merge.

Using an embroidery hoop

For painting designs on a small scale, and also for embroidery, you may need to stretch the fabric to get the best result. A wooden embroidery hoop is the most popular method of stretching fabric.

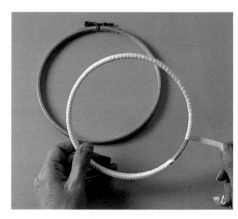

1 For embroidery, to protect the fabric wrap a length of 5mm/¼in-wide seam tape round the inside ring at a slight angle so that the tape overlaps all the way round. Fold the raw edge to the inside of the hoop and hem stitch.

If you are using an embroidery hoop for painting, wrap the inside ring with masking tape to protect the frame from the paint dyes.

2 Remove the outer frame. Place the required area of the fabric, right side up, over the inner hoop. Loosen the tension ring slightly. Hold the outer ring in place and push it down to secure the fabric between the rings. Pull the fabric taut in all directions and tighten the screw slightly. Use a screwdriver to tighten the outer hoop to keep the tension taut.

Masking

Masking tape adhered to fabric will prevent paint from penetrating defined areas of the fabric.

1 Stick strips of masking tape to dry fabric that has been stretched taut. Ensure that there are no gaps in the tape or the paint will seep through. Ensure that the tape is firmly adhered to the fabric to prevent paint from seeping underneath. Leave the paint to dry before removing the tape.

Paint this colourful sofa throw freehand so that all the flower pots are different and the result looks spontaneous and creative. Decorate it with simple machine and hand stitching to add to the textured effect.

Flower Pot Throw

you will need

paper and pencil

tailor's chalk

large piece of thick cotton cloth

cardboard

fabric paints in dark blue, light blue, olive green, pink, red and mauve

palette and sponges

wide masking tape

medium artist's paintbrush

sewing machine

sewing thread

embroidery thread (floss) in contrast colours

embroidery needle

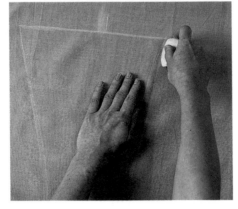

1 Plan your design on plain paper first, so that you know how many flower pots will fit along the length of the fabric. Using tailor's chalk, draw a large, simple flower pot shape on the fabric. Alternatively, cut one out of paper and draw around it if you prefer. Position it at a jaunty angle.

2 Position a piece of cardboard underneath the fabric to protect the work surface. Empty a small quantity of fabric paint into a palette, and dilute as required. Using a sponge, apply dark blue fabric paint to fill in the flower pot, taking care not to splash outside the outline.

3 When the paint has dried, stick strips of wide masking tape across the flowerpot in bands to mark out the stripes on the flower pot. The stripes do not need to be parallel.

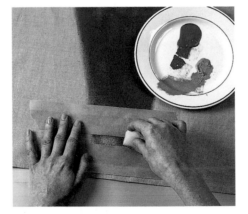

4 Using a smaller sponge, apply light blue fabric paint to colour the stripes, between the strips of tape. Allow to dry, then carefully remove the masking tape.

5 Using a paintbrush, paint an olive green vertical line for the flower's stem. Add some freehand leaves using the same colour.

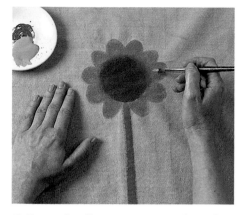

6 Paint the flower centre pink, red or mauve, then paint the petals. Leave all the paints to dry thoroughly.

7 To define the shape, decorate the flower pot with machine embroidery using a complementary colour.

8 Machine stitch details on the stem and leaves, and around the petals in the same way.

9 Using contrast embroidery thread (floss), hand embroider French knots in the flower centre. Repeat the design all over the fabric, placing the flower pots at different angles.

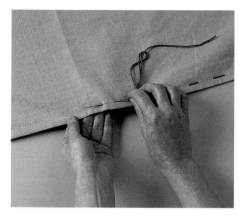

10 Press under a narrow double hem around all sides of the throw. Using thick embroidery thread or several strands in the needle, work large running stitches around the hemline to secure the hem in place.

Make this fun fashion accessory for a pet who likes to show off! Paint your own motifs freehand or use traditional spots or stripes for a smart effect. Scale the measurements up or down to suit the size of your pet.

Pet's Bow Tie

you will need

30cm/12in square of white cotton fabric

small embroidery hoop

soft pencil

ruler

gold outliner pen

fabric paint pens in various colours, to suit your design

scissors

20cm/8in square of coloured cotton fabric

dressmaker's pins and needle

sewing machine (optional)

matching sewing threads

2 small pieces of Velcro

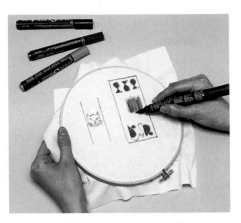

1 Fit the white fabric into the embroidery hoop. Using a pencil and ruler, mark a rectangle 7.5 x 14cm/3 x 5½in for the bow, and another rectangle 10 x 4cm/4 x 1½in for the central band. Draw a design freehand on each rectangle then paint over it with a gold outliner pen. Leave to dry.

2 Using fabric paint pens, fill in the design. Apply colour just outside the rectangles. Leave the paints to dry. Cut out both rectangles, leaving a 1.5cm/⅝in seam allowance all round. Cut rectangles to the same size from the coloured fabric.

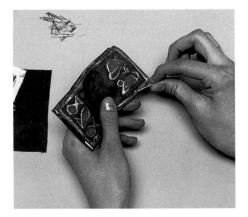

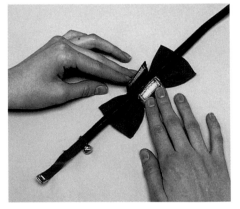

3 Fold under 1.5cm/⅝in on the edges of the painted rectangle to the wrong side, and 1cm/½in on the coloured rectangles. Pin the rectangles wrong sides together, and hand or machine stitch around the edges. Repeat for the central band.

4 Work two rows of running stitch down the middle of the bow tie. Gather up the running stitches. Stitch the central band over the gathers. Stitch each half of Velcro to each end of the central band. Use the remaining Velcro to attach the bow around your pet's collar.

Paint this sheer fabric freehand with simple leaf shapes, then add machine-embroidered details over the top. The fabric is held taut in an embroidery hoop for both the painting and the embroidery.

Leaf-painted Organza Scarf

you will need

silk organza or chiffon

embroidery hoop

fine artist's paintbrush

fabric paints in green and blue

plate

iron

sewing machine, with a darning foot

machine embroidery threads (floss) in orange and red

scissors

needle

matching sewing thread

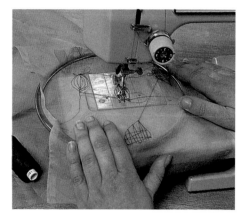

1 Wash and dry the silk to remove any dressing. Stretch the fabric taut in an embroidery hoop. Paint leaf shapes freehand in green and blue, mixing the paints to achieve subtle tones. Allow to dry before moving the hoop along the fabric. Iron to fix (set) the paints, using a warm, dry iron.

2 Select the darning or free-stitch mode on your sewing machine and attach a darning foot. Replace the fabric in the embroidery hoop. Machine stitch details in orange and red embroidery threads over the painted leaves, moving the hoop along the fabric as you work.

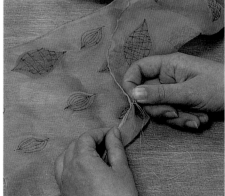

3 Trim the raw edges of the fabric. Roll under a small hem on each side in turn and slip stitch by hand, using matching thread.

Varnished floorcloths were introduced to America by European settlers, as a means of adding colour to the home. Artist's suppliers sell canvas in a wide range of sizes, pre-primed, or you can prime it yourself.

Stars-and-stripes Floorcloth

you will need

natural-coloured artist's canvas

ruler and pencil

craft knife and cutting mat

5cm/2in-wide double-sided carpet tape

white acrylic primer (optional)

medium decorator's brush

masking tape

acrylic paints in scarlet, cobalt blue and white

plate

tracing paper

spray adhesive (stencil mount)

stencil card (card stock)

stencil brush

clear or antique tinted matt (flat) polyurethane varnish

varnish brush

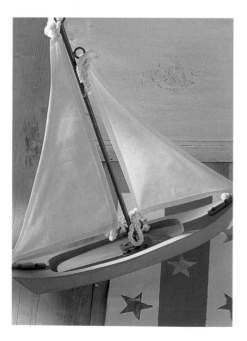

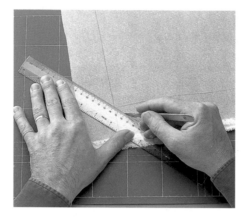

1 Draw a 10cm/4in border on all four sides of the back of the canvas. Using a craft knife, cut diagonally across the corners. Stick double-sided carpet tape along the drawn border. Peel off the backing, then fold the raw edge in to create a neat edge.

2 If the canvas is unprimed, apply two coats of acrylic primer. Leave the primer to dry between coats. Using the pencil and ruler, mark vertical stripes 7.5cm/3in wide down the length of the canvas. Outline alternating stripes with masking tape.

3 Paint the alternating canvas stripes with scarlet acrylic paint.

4 Leave the paint to dry, then peel off the masking tape.

5 Trace the star from the back of the book and enlarge as required. Spray the back lightly with adhesive and stick on to stencil card (card stock). Accurately cut out the star template, using a craft knife.

6 Place the stencil on a white stripe, 5cm/2in from one end. Using a stencil brush, apply blue paint, working in from the points of the star. Wipe the back of the stencil to avoid smudging. Space the stars 10cm/4in apart.

7 Repeat with white paint on the scarlet stripes, positioning the white stars to fall halfway between the blue stars. Apply at least three coats of varnish. An antique tinted varnish will mellow the bright colours.

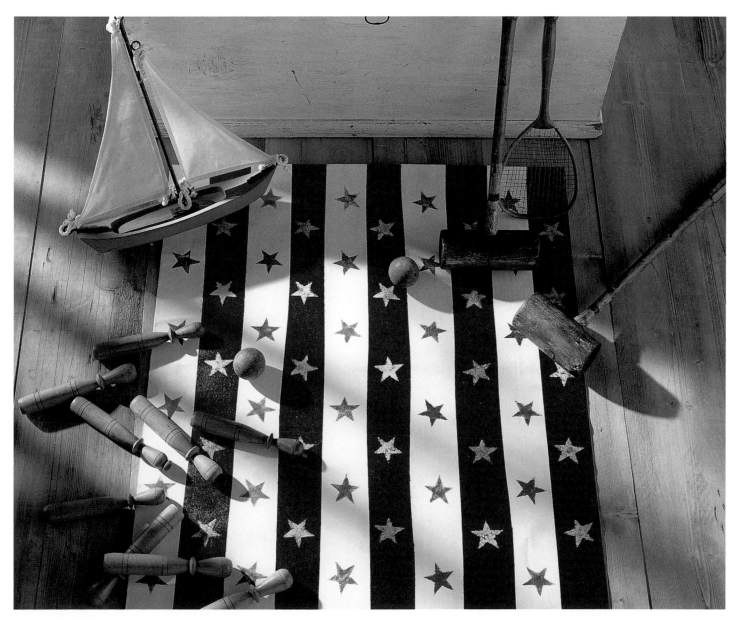

Paint exuberant dots, circles and swirls on the front of this cushion, then decorate it with simple stitches and buttons in contrast colours. Finish with a row of buttons along the back.

Polka Dot Cushion

you will need

scissors

40cm/16in of 90cm/36in-wide white linen fabric

30cm/12in of 90cm/36in-wide coloured linen fabric

dressmaker's pins

sewing machine

matching sewing thread

fabric paints in various colours

paint palette

medium artist's paintbrush

iron

embroidery thread (floss)

embroidery needle

assortment of coloured buttons

2m/2yd of 4cm/1½in-wide contrast fabric, for the piping

2m/2yd piping cord

tacking (basting) thread

Velcro

cushion pad, to fit the finished cover

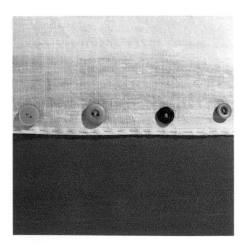

1 From the white linen cut a 40cm/ 16in square for the cushion front, and 41 x 23cm/16½ x 9in rectangle for the back. From the coloured linen, cut a 41 x 30cm/16½ x 12in rectangle for the back. Fold over 1cm/½in of one 41cm/16½in edge on each back piece to make a hem. Pin, then machine stitch in place.

2 Place the front of the cushion on a flat, covered surface. Using fabric paints and a paintbrush, paint free-hand circles, dots and swirls. Leave the fabric to dry between each colour so that the paint does not smudge and discolour. Allow to dry, then fix (set) the paints following the manufacturer's instructions.

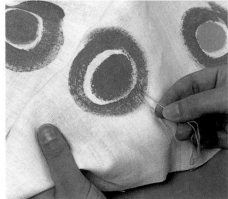

3 Decorate the painted design with circles of running stitches in contrast-coloured embroidery threads (floss).

Left: The back of the cushion is finished with different size buttons in bright colours.

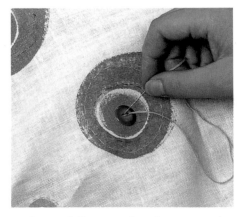

4 Sew a different colour button in the centre of each circle.

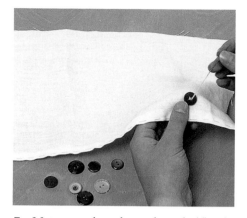 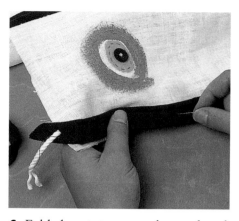 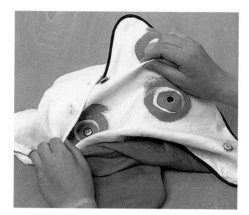

5 Using embroidery thread (floss), work running stitch along the hem of the white cushion back. Sew a line of buttons above the running stitch.

6 Fold the piping over the cord and stitch. Pin to the cushion front, raw edges aligned. Place the cushion backs on the front, right sides together.

7 Using a zipper foot, stitch close to the piping. Turn the cover right side out. Press. Sew Velcro to each side of the opening. Insert the cushion pad.

Silver metallic paint and delicate chiffon combine to make a beautiful scarf for a special occasion. The motifs are finished with rows of dots, using a nozzle-tipped fabric paint dispenser.

Wild Rose Chiffon Scarf

you will need

30 x 50cm/12 x 20in piece of silk chiffon

iron

drawing pins or assa pins (push pins)

wooden painting frame

tracing paper and pencil

silver metallic fabric paint

paint container

fine artist's paintbrush

metallic paint in nozzle-tip dispenser

vanishing fabric marker

needle

scissors

1 Fold the chiffon in quarters, and press with a warm iron, then fold the rectangle diagonally and press again to leave guidelines for the design. Unfold the chiffon.

2 Using drawing pins or assa pins (push pins), stretch and pin the fabric over the painting frame, pulling the fabric taut. The guidelines should still be visible and the fabric should feel slightly stretchy. The pins will mark delicate fabric, but the edges of the scarf will be lost in the fringe.

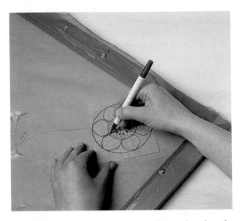

3 Enlarge the rose motif at the back of the book. Trace it on to the back of the fabric, placing it in the centre using the central fold as a guide. Trace eight more rose motifs in a circle around the first, again using the ironed fold lines as a guide.

4 Turn the frame over. Working on the front of the fabric, outline the roses with silver metallic fabric paint, using a fine paintbrush. Leave the paint to dry. Remove the chiffon from the frame and iron it on a cool heat to fix (set) the paint, following the manufacturer's instructions. Replace the chiffon in the frame, pinning it taut.

5 Make dots of metallic paint around the outline of each rose and then fill in the details. Mark a line 5cm/2in from the edge of the fabric on all four sides, using a vanishing fabric marker. Fray the edges of the scarf. Use a needle to separate and remove threads from the raw edges up to the line. Tidy the ends of the fringe with scissors.

Evoke the charm of country-style table linen with this traditional heart design. Work the motif in one corner of a set of napkins. The open weave linen threads make it easier to position the crosses neatly.

Cross Stitch Monograms

you will need

iron

52cm/21in square of linen for each napkin

ruler

tailor's chalk

scissors and seam ripper

sewing machine and sewing thread

tracing paper and pencil

dressmaker's pins

carbon tracing paper

large embroidery needle

tablespoon and teaspoon

cerise fabric paint

fabric medium

fine artist's paintbrush

cotton embroidery thread (floss) to match the paint colour, 1 skein for every 2 napkins

1 Using a hot iron, press under a 1cm/½in hem on all sides of each linen square. Measure 2.5cm/1in from each corner along the edge and mark with tailor's chalk. Cut the corners off across the markings, then open out the folds. Fold the fabric across the diagonal. Align the cut corners and stitch across the cut edge.

2 Turn the corner out and ease out the point with the blunt end of a seam ripper. Similarly treat the other three corners. On the wrong side of the napkin, press all the new hems that have been created by mitring the corners. Stitch the hems in place 1cm/½in in from the pressed edge. Make as many napkins as desired.

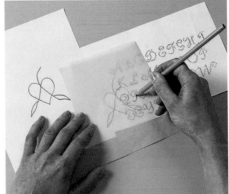

3 Trace the heart template from the back of the book. Trace the required letters for your monogram on each side of the heart. Position and size the letters carefully as this will affect the look of the finished design.

4 Place the tracing on a corner of a napkin. Slip a piece of carbon tracing paper under the tracing, chalk-side down. Pin in place. With a needle, prick through the layers of paper, making close holes along the lines of the design to transfer it to the fabric.

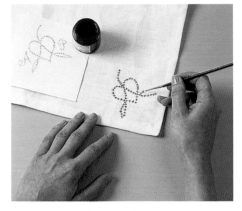

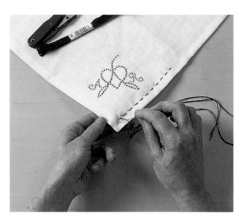

5 Mix a tablespoonful of cerise paint with a teaspoonful of fabric medium. Using a paintbrush and following the lines of the transfer, carefully paint in a series of small "x"s to give the illusion of cross stitch.

6 Use a piece of scrap fabric to practise the "x"s and monogram and also to clean off any excess paint from the paintbrush. Complete the design and leave to dry.

7 Using three strands of embroidery thread (floss), sew running stitch over the sewn hem on each napkin. Using a warm, dry iron, press each napkin to fix (set) the paint, following the manufacturer's instructions.

Jazz up a plain fabric lampshade with hand-drawn stripes of colour, using oil pastel sticks, then decorate the bottom edge with oversized cotton pompoms.

Striped Pompom Lampshade

you will need

pencil

white lampshade

oil pastel sticks

cardboard

pair of compasses (compass)

scissors

cotton yarn, in 5 colours

selection of 5mm/¼in-wide ribbons

large needle

ceramic paints

fine or medium artist's paintbrush

white ceramic lamp base

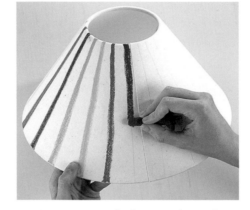

1 Using a pencil, draw 20 lines from the top edge of the shade to the bottom, spacing them evenly around the bottom circumference. Draw thick lines over the pencil marks, using different shades of oil pastels. Leave for at least 24 hours to dry.

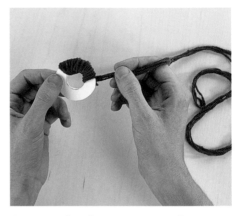

2 To make the pompoms, draw two circles each 6.5cm/2½in-diameter on a piece of cardboard. Draw a 2.5cm/1in diameter circle inside the centre of each one. Cut around the outer and inner circles. Holding the two circles together, wrap cotton yarn around them until the central hole is full.

3 Place one blade of the scissors between the two pieces of card and cut the yarn. Tie a length of ribbon around the centre, between the two cards. Pull one side of the pompom through the holes to remove the cards. Fluff out the yarn. Make ten pompoms, using different colours.

4 Using a large needle, punch ten holes around the bottom of the shade to correspond with alternate stripes. Thread one end of the ribbon around each pompom through a hole from the outside. Knot the ends. Paint stripes of colour around the lamp base, using ceramic paints. Leave to dry.

The softly blurred edges of this simple masked-out grid look very attractive, especially when daylight filters through the unlined fabric. The fabric paints are specially thickened to achieve this effect.

Checked Café Curtain

you will need

white silk dupion

iron

tape measure or ruler

2.5cm/1in-wide masking tape

fabric paints in yellow, orange and pink

gum thickener or anti-spread

medium artist's paintbrushes

wooden frame

silk pins (push pins)

dressmaker's pins

sewing machine

sewing thread

2.5cm/1in-wide ribbon

1 Wash the fabric to remove any finish and press flat. Cut the fabric 1½–2 times the width of the window plus seam allowances. Add seam allowances to the length for the top and bottom. Apply masking tape to make evenly spaced horizontal stripes.

2 Mix the fabric paints with thickener or anti-spread. Stretch the fabric across a wooden frame. Hold it in place with silk pins (push pins).

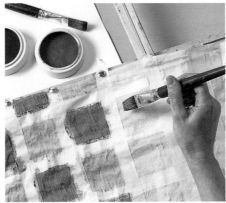

4 Apply vertical lengths of masking tape to the fabric to make evenly spaced squares. Paint alternate squares pink and orange. Leave to dry. Carefully remove the tape. The areas which were taped will have soft edges where the paint has seeped through. Set (fix) the paints by prolonged ironing with a warm dry iron, following the manufacturer's instructions.

3 Using a paintbrush, apply thickened yellow paint in even strokes. Leave to dry.

5 Wash the fabric in warm water to remove the thickener. Fold and pin a narrow hem across the top and down the sides. Machine stitch in place with matching thread. Turn under 5cm/2in along the top of the curtain and press. Cut lengths of ribbon to make loops for hanging. Fold them in half, and space them evenly along the tape lines. Pin, then stitch each in place. Turn up the bottom hem of the curtain to the required length.

Rich velvet fabric, painted gold, creates a magnificent effect, but the hand-drawn oval motif also makes this screen look contemporary. Three shades of red velvet are used to create a subtle effect.

Gold-painted Velvet Screen

you will need

scissors

silk-rayon velvet, in three slightly different shades of red

ready-made three-panel screen

old blanket

masking tape

plastic sheet

tailor's chalk

medium decorator's paintbrush

gold fabric paint

iron

protective goggles

staple gun

tape measure

petersham ribbon

PVA (white) glue and brush

piano hinges and screwdriver

1 Cut two shades of velvet for each screen panel – one for each side – leaving a generous margin on all sides. Cover the work surface with a blanket and tape a plastic sheet on top. Stretch the velvet panels taut; tape them right side up to the work surface, keeping the fabric grain straight.

2 Using tailor's chalk, draw large ovals on the velvet. Draw some ovals so that they disappear off the sides of the panels. Fill in the ovals with gold paint. Do not load the brush too heavily, as the paint spreads well and the effect is enhanced by having slightly broken colour.

3 When the paint is thoroughly dry, carefully untape the velvet panels. Following the manufacturer's instructions, iron each panel on the back to fix (set) the paint.

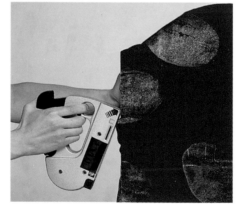

4 Wearing protective goggles, staple a painted length of velvet to the front and back of each screen panel, pulling the fabric taut and working from side to side towards the centre. Measure the top, one side and the bottom of a side panel.

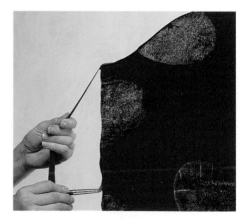

5 Cut two pieces of petersham ribbon to this length, plus 6cm/2½in. Cut two lengths of ribbon for the top and bottom edges of the centre panel. Spread glue along the edges of the panels and press the ribbon in place, turning under the ends. Hinge the panels together using a screwdriver.

Paint freehand stripes on a plain shade, highlighting some of them with sponged gold paint. Alternatively, use strips of masking tape to stencil out the unpainted areas.

Multi-textured Lampshade

you will need
felt-tipped pen
plain cotton lampshade
paints in various colours,
including gold
medium artist's paintbrush
small sponge
masking tape
scissors
velvet ribbons in various colours
fabric glue and brush

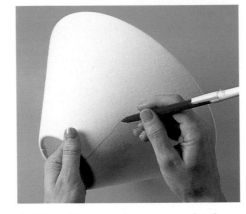

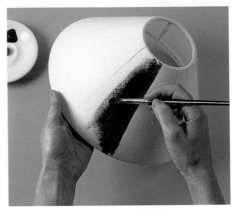

1 Use a felt-tipped pen to mark where the stripes are to be painted on the lampshade. Use a tape measure, if you wish, to help space the lines.

2 Using a variety of fabric paints, paint stripes on to the lampshade. Leave to dry.

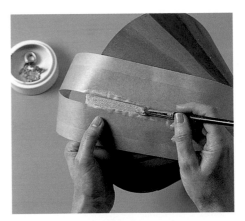

3 To highlight some of the stripes with gold fabric paint, use a small sponge and dab on small amounts of gold paint. Build the colour up gradually rather than loading the sponge with paint.

4 For more precise stripes, apply strips of masking tape to the lampshade to serve as stencils.

5 Using a paintbrush, apply fabric paints in contrast colours between the pieces of tape.

6 Leave to dry completely, then remove the tape carefully to reveal the stripes.

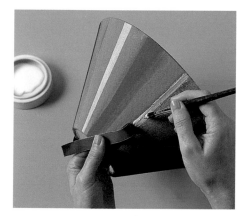

7 Cut lengths of velvet ribbon slightly longer than the depth of the lampshade. Apply fabric glue to the back and press in place.

8 Fold over the ends of the ribbon to the inside at the top and bottom of the shade. Glue in place, pulling taut and leave to dry.

The red painted border of this traditional American floorcloth is coated with coloured vinegar glaze, and the glaze is then repeated over the centre panel. Use homemade stamps to decorate the wet glaze.

Vinegar-glazed Floorcloth

you will need

heavyweight cotton duck canvas, 7.5cm/3in larger all round than the finished floorcloth

staple gun or hammer and tacks

white acrylic wood primer

large and medium decorator's paintbrushes

fine-grade sandpaper

set square (t-square)

large scissors

pencil

PVA (white) glue and brush

2.5cm/1in-wide masking tape

dessertspoon

bright red emulsion (latex) paint

gloss or matt (flat) acrylic floor varnish

varnish brush

1cm/½in-wide masking tape

malt vinegar

sugar

bowl and spoon

dark ultramarine powder pigment

reusable tacky adhesive

craft knife

cork

dark shellac and brush

1 Stretch the canvas over a large work surface and staple or tack in place. Paint with three or four coats of primer, leaving to dry between coats, then sand to give a smooth surface.

2 Using a set square (t-square), check that the canvas is square, and trim if not. Mark a pencil border 2.5cm/1in from the edge. Cut diagonally across each corner, through the point where the pencil lines cross.

3 Fold over each edge to the pencil line. Glue, then secure with masking tape until dry. Rub the edges firmly with a dessertspoon to seal the layers together. Sand the edges where the primer has cracked.

4 Turn the canvas to the right side. Using masking tape, mark a wide border. Paint the border area with red emulsion (latex) paint. Allow to dry, then apply a coat of floor varnish. Leave to dry.

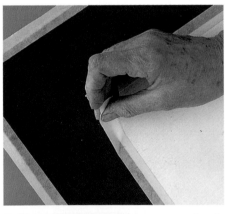

5 Remove the masking tape and tidy any ragged edges with extra paint. When dry, place 1cm/½in-wide tape around the outer edge to a depth of 1cm/½in. Repeat around the inner edge of the border.

6 Mix 150ml/¼ pint/⅔ cup malt vinegar with 5ml/1 tsp sugar. Add up to 30ml/2 tbsp of dark ultramarine pigment and stir well. Paint the glaze evenly over the red border.

7 While the ultramarine glaze is still wet, make patterns by pressing the reusable tacky adhesive on top and then removing it. The glaze will take about 15 minutes to dry.

8 Use the reusable tacky adhesive to make additional lines and curves. Leave to dry. Cut a hole in one end of the cork. Paint the ultramarine glaze over the centre panel.

9 While it is still wet, stamp a pattern of circles and lines with the cork. Cut a square at the other end of the cork to make a different stamp.

10 Remove the tape. Apply a coat of shellac, then several coats of varnish, allowing the canvas to dry between each. Leave for 4 days before using.

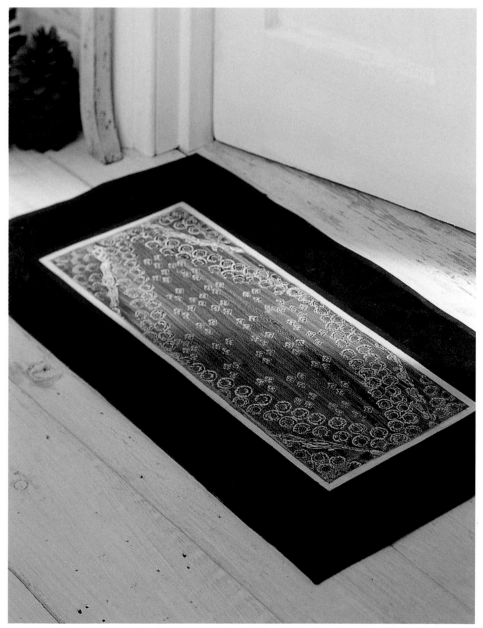

Painting on Silk

Silk is the ideal fabric to work with. It absorbs paints and dyes beautifully, and there is a special range of transparent iron-fix (set) paints designed to give lovely clear colours. Create finely drawn designs using gutta – an outline that creates a barrier to prevent the paint from spreading – or experiment with abstract effects by adding unusual materials such as salt and bleach.

Hand-crafted Art

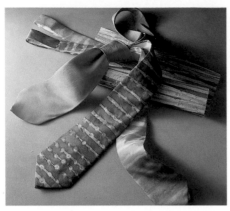

Archaeological evidence tells us that silk was culti-vated in China as early as 3200BC, using the finest silkworm caterpillars fed on the best mulberry leaves. The Chinese kept the making of this luxury fabric a closely guarded secret, trading silk with other countries, at a high price for precious stones and metals. Eventually silk reached the Roman Empire, which at first paid out-rageous prices for this highly desirable fabric and led to the opening of the famous "Silk Road" via northern India.

Silk is the most beautiful of all fabrics and an ideal surface for painting on.

Its sensual feel, lustre and ability to absorb colour have inspired artists throughout the centuries. It is available in different weights, from floating geor-gette and chiffon to heavy Habotai or pongee, so you can choose the ideal fabric for each project.

A range of transparent iron-fix (set) silk paints has been specially designed for use with silk alone. The colours are set by heat, so you can use an iron or a hairdryer, which is useful for projects such as a parasol where ironing would

be impractical. To draw precise designs on silk, transparent or coloured gutta is often used as a resist to prevent the paint from flowing across the fabric into unwanted areas. The transparent gutta is removed at the end by hand washing, while the coloured gutta remains on the fabric as part of the finished design. Wash silk by hand with a mild detergent and press it on the reverse side while it is still damp.

If you are not a proficient artist, you can draw a design first on paper or trace one of the templates at the back of the book, then transfer it on to the

silk using a vanishing fabric marker. Wonderful effects can also be created by sprinkling different kinds of salt on to the damp silk paints.

Another technique is to remove the colour from pre-dyed silk with bleach, dotted over the surface with a paintbrush, which gives a subtle effect and different colour density. Finally, machine or hand embroidery threads will add further three-dimensional texture to your individually painted work of art.

Although any fabric paint can be used on silk, specially formulated silk paints are the best choice. Many weights and types of silk can be used, with medium-weight habotai silk a good choice for beginners.

Materials

Paper
Silk paints can be fixed by placing each painted area between sheets of paper and ironing.

Powder dye
Fabrics can be pre-dyed using hot or cold powder dyes.

Salt
Add to damp silk paint to distort the colours. Brush off after use.

Silk
Available in different weights. Crêpe de chine, chiffon and georgette are ideal for lightweight items. Habotai or pongee silk varies in weight and has a smooth, soft sheen, as does silk-satin.

Sticky-backed plastic (Contact paper)
Attach to thin cardboard stencils and cut out to stick temporarily on to fabric to resist the paint.

Thickener
Mix into silk paints to prevent them from spreading. Thickened paint is used for painting details.

Watercolours or coloured inks
Useful for preparing designs on paper as they have the same quality as transparent silk paints on silk. Their strong colours can easily be seen through silk.

Anti-spreading agent
Starch-like liquid applied to fabric to prevent the paints from spreading. Remove by hand washing.

Batik wax
Can be used to resist silk paints. Heat the wax in a double boiler or wax pot.

Bleach
Apply to pre-dyed fabric to remove the colour. Wash out immediately.

Gutta
Gel-like substance used with an applicator to draw a design on silk. It acts as a barrier to the paint. Remove transparent gutta by hand washing.

Iron-fix (set) silk paints
These paints are specially designed for use on silk. They are fixed (set) by direct heat, such as an iron or a hairdryer. Steam-fix dyes are also available, and are fixed with steam.

Silk painting does require specialist equipment, but most of it is quite inexpensive. The most important pieces you will need are a wooden painting frame and silk pins to hold the delicate fabric on the frame.

Equipment

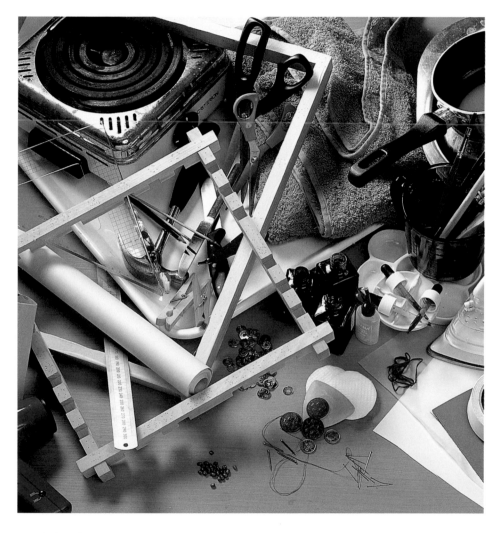

Paint palette
Use to hold and mix paint colours.

Paintbrushes
Use a decorator's paintbrush to paint large areas. Use a medium paintbrush to paint a design, and a fine paintbrush for details. Use a sponge brush to dampen silk before painting and to apply paint or anti-spreading agent. Use a toothbrush to spray paint.

Pens and pencils
Use a black marker pen to draw on the acetate sheet. Use a soft pencil to trace templates.

Silk-painting frame
Make your own wooden frame to stretch silk taut ready for painting.

Silk pins (push pins)
Use special flat-headed pins with three points to attach silk to a frame.

Sponge
A natural sponge can be used to apply paint, e.g. around stencils.

Staple gun
Use to mount a picture in a frame.

Tailor's chalk/Fabric marker
Use to temporarily mark designs on to the fabric.

Craft knife
Use to cut stencils. Always use with a cutting mat.

Double boiler or wax pot
Use to melt batik wax.

Gutta applicator
Fitted with various-size nibs (tips) for drawing a design on to silk to resist the paint. Fill no more than three-quarters full for even, flowing paint.

Hairdryer
Use to fix (set) iron-fix silk paints.

Iron
Use to press the fabric, and to make iron-fix silk paint permanent.

Masking tape
Use to mask off areas of the design.

Needle
Use for hand stitching.

Silk fibres normally contain dressing that looks slightly oily. It needs to be removed from the silk before painting or dyeing so that the colours can penetrate the fibres. To remove the dressing, hand wash the silk in warm, soapy water, using a mild detergent. Dry it by hanging it on a line, or roll it in a towel to remove excess water. Press while damp. Some objects, such as fans and umbrellas, are unwashable, and these should be painted by incorporating a thickener into the paint. Start with a simple project and practise with the silk paints first.

Techniques

Making a frame

Several different kinds of silk-painting frame are available for purchase, the adjustable ones being the most useful.

1 Cut four pieces of planed timber or battening to make a frame. The frame should be slightly larger than the finished piece, to allow for trimming untidy fabric edges. Using wood adhesive, glue two pieces together to form a right angle. Repeat with the remaining two pieces and leave the adhesive to dry.

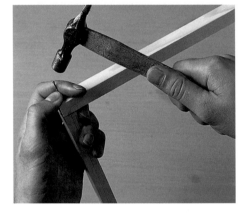

◄ 2 When the adhesive has set, glue the two right angles together to form the frame. Leave the glue to dry, then tap a panel pin (tack) into each joint to hold it firmly.

Pinning silk to a frame

Silk should be pulled taut on a frame and be springy to the touch before it is painted on, to ensure an even coverage of paint.

1 Use three-pronged silk pins to attach the silk to the frame. Place the first pin in the centre of one edge and work out towards each corner.

2 Space the pins an equal distance apart. Pull the silk over the frame and pin the opposite edge, placing the pins directly opposite each other.

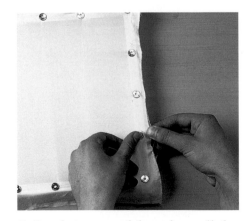

3 Pin down one of the sides, pull the silk taut across the frame, and then pin the final side. The silk should be springy, without being too tight.

Paint effects

Iron-fix (set) silk paints are available in a wide range of colours and are specially designed for use with silk.

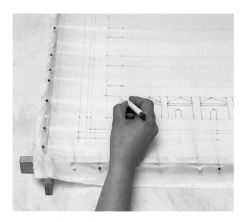

1 On fine silks place a traced design underneath the frame and copy over it with a vanishing marker pen.

2 Or, turn the frame upside down and trace the design with a pencil. On the right side, trace the lines with gutta.

3 Mix paints together to achieve the exact shade required. Ensure you have enough of each for the whole design.

4 A single paint colour mixed with white produces a delicate pastel tone. Continue adding white until you achieve the desired colour.

5 Paints can be diluted with water to make a wash. This is most often used to fill a background. Use a large brush to apply the diluted paint quickly over a large area.

6 Paints will bleed into each other if applied quickly before they dry. Use a soft brush and flowing movements.

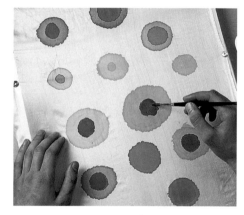

7 If a colour is applied over another, while the first paint is damp, they will merge and give a soft, blurred effect.

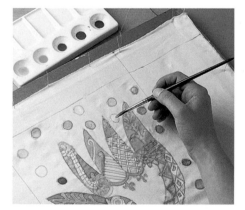

8 When using gutta, dot paint in the centre of each outlined shape and it will quickly spread to the gutta lines.

9 Use a large brush to fill large areas quickly (sponge brush or paint brush). This will stop watermarks from appearing. Use a fine brush for details.

10 Use a cotton wool ball held between tweezers or a clothes peg (pin) to create a softer tool where no definition is required.

Using gutta

Gutta is a thin, gel-like substance that acts as a barrier against paints, isolating areas of colour. It is applied to the fabric using an applicator that can be fitted with a detachable nib (tip) according to the fineness of line required. Do not fill the applicator more than three-quarters full and squeeze gently. Alternatively, purchase gutta in ready-to-use tubes.

Gutta is available in various colours, as well as transparent. Transparent guttas wash out, but coloured ones need to be fixed (set) and remain as part of the finished design. When working with gutta, it is essential to use special silk paints, as ordinary fabric paints contain binders that leave the colour opaque and can stiffen the fabric.

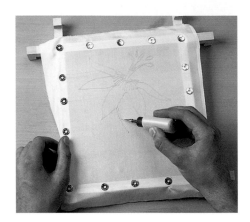

1 Place the covered frame upside down on the design and trace the pattern on to the back of the fabric, using a soft pencil. This will reverse the design; if you wish the design to be the original way round, transfer it first on to tracing paper.

2 Working on the right side of the silk, go over the design outline with gutta. It is important to maintain a continuous line, otherwise the paints will be able to seep through. Turn the silk over from time to time to check the back. Here, the applicator is fitted with a fine detachable nib (tip). Leave to dry.

3 When the gutta is dry, apply the silk paints in the centre of each defined area. Keep the brushstrokes light, allowing the colour to bleed from the brush outwards to the gutta lines. If the paint breaks through the gutta line there is no way to remedy the situation, except by washing the silk and starting again.

Fixing (setting) silk paints

Iron-fix (set) silk paints are made permanent by the use of heat, either by ironing the fabric or by using a hairdryer.

1 When the painting is complete, leave the paints to dry.

▸**2** Remove the finished piece from the frame and fix (set) the paints, following the manufacturer's instructions, usually by pressing with a warm, dry iron on the wrong side.

3 Alternatively, use a hairdryer set on a high setting to fix (set) a piece of silk that is still mounted on a silk-painting frame, or if the object would be difficult to iron.

4 Wash out transparent guttas by hand, using a mild detergent.

Using thickeners

There are two types of thickener, both of which are used to prevent the silk paints from spreading into unwanted areas of the design. Thickener allows you to paint without flooding the fabric. It is used on objects that cannot be pre-washed, or where you are working with a stencil and do not want the paint to seep underneath. Thickened paint is mostly used for painting small areas and to add details to some designs. Mix thickener into the paints by placing both together in a screw-top jar with a lid and shaking vigorously.

1 Use thickener for painting small areas and to add details.

2 Alternatively apply anti-spreading agent to the silk before painting.

Using salt

Designs can be created by sprinkling salt or dabbing bleach on to the surface of the fabric while the paints are damp. Adding salt to damp silk paint will distort the paint, giving a lovely mottled effect. Different salts will produce different results, so experiment with different kinds. It is important that the paint is still damp when you add the salt, so alternate painting and applying salt. Leave the finished design to dry naturally, then gently rub off the salt crystals.

1 Add rock salt grains with tweezers.

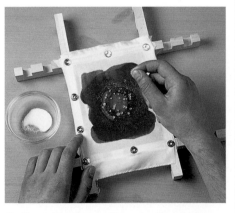

2 Sprinkle fine salt over the surface.

Using bleach

Remove the colour from pre-dyed silk by bleaching using a brush.

Dye the silk as desired, following the manufacturer's instructions. Apply the bleach a little at a time until you get the desired effect. Wash the silk immediately to remove the bleach, otherwise it will rot the fabric.

Transform a small silk umbrella into an exquisite parasol by adding a freehand design outlined with dots of metallic fabric paint. Open the umbrella while you are working so that the silk is stretched taut.

Summer Parasol

you will need

small plain silk umbrella

sponge brush

fabric paints in 4 colours, including

metallic

hairdryer

tailor's chalk

fine artist's paintbrushes

1 Apply a background colour to some or all of the umbrella panels. Dampen the silk using a sponge brush soaked in water then apply the paint using the sponge brush. Fix (set) the paint with a hairdryer used on a high heat.

2 Using tailor's chalk, draw your choice of design on to the umbrella. Refer to the template provided. Using a paintbrush, apply dots of metallic paint along some of the tailor's chalk outlines. Allow to dry.

3 Paint a line along one edge of some of the chalked leaves. Paint in the details of the leaves in a contrasting colour. Add simple stylized flowers as desired. Leave to dry. Remove the tailor's chalk by brushing the surface lightly. Fix the paint using the heat of a hairdryer.

Delicate crêpe de chine, painted with squares of soft colour, makes a beautiful modern room divider. The silk paints make the fabric opaque, so leaving some squares unpainted creates a subtle contrast.

Chequered Screen

you will need

scissors

cream silk crêpe de chine, pre-washed

open-panel screen

old blanket

masking tape

plastic sheet

tailor's chalk pencil

ruler

medium decorator's paintbrush

iron-fix (set) silk paints, in soft colours

iron

sewing machine

matching sewing thread

curtain wire

screw eyes and metal hooks

two pairs of cabinet hinges

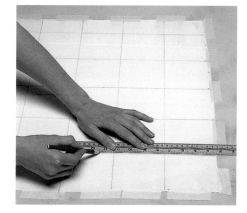

1 Cut a panel of silk to fit each frame of the screen, allowing extra for the casings and hems and for the ruched effect. Protect the work surface with a blanket, and tape the plastic over the top. Stretch the first silk panel taut and tape it to the work surface. Using a tailor's chalk pencil and ruler, divide each panel into squares.

2 Place strips of masking tape around the edges of certain squares. Using a decorator's paintbrush, fill in the squares with the silk paints. Leave some squares unpainted.

3 Leave the paint to dry, then remove the masking tape. Iron the back of the silk, following the manufacturer's instructions, to fix (set) the colours.

4 Hem the edges of each panel, then make a narrow casing at the top and bottom. Attach lengths of curtain wire to the top and bottom of each frame, using screw eyes and metal hooks. Hinge the screen together, and slip the panels on to the curtain wire.

Trace this pretty flower motif on to a delicate silk camisole or pyjama top, then paint it in a soft pastel colour. Simple machine embroidery stitches complete the fresh, natural design.

Flowery Camisole

you will need

tracing paper and pencil

white paper

silk camisole, pre-washed

shallow cardboard box

vanishing fabric marker

silk pins (push pins)

transparent gutta and applicator

fine artist's paintbrush

paint palette

small bowl

iron-fix (set) silk paints, in 1 colour and white

iron

sewing machine

metallic thread

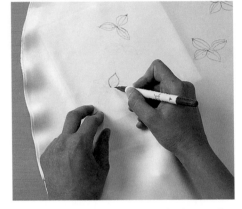

1 Trace the floral motifs from the back of the book on to a sheet of paper. Separate the two sides of the camisole by placing a shallow cardboard box inside. Insert the paper on top of the box and trace several flowers on to the outside of the camisole, using a vanishing fabric marker.

2 To make the silk taut, pin the camisole to the sides of the box, through the seams or hem only, using silk pins. Smooth out any wrinkles. Apply transparent gutta along the outlines of the design, making sure there are no gaps in the line. Leave the gutta to dry thoroughly.

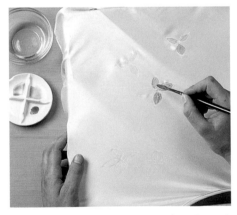

3 Using a fine artist's paintbrush and a paint palette, mix the coloured paint with white until you achieve the desired tone. Apply the paint within the gutta outline. Allow the paint to dry thoroughly, then unpin the silk from the box.

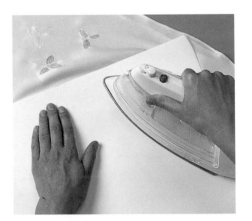

4 To fix (set) the colour, place each painted area between two sheets of white paper and press using a warm, dry iron, following the manufacturer's instructions. Hand wash the camisole to remove the gutta.

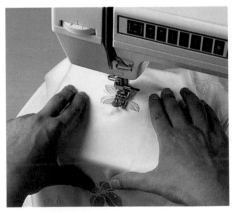

5 Thread a sewing machine with metallic thread. Holding the fabric taut with your hands, stitch two straight lines as a stem for each flower. Add any other details you like.

Paint the background to this flowing design very loosely so that the colours bleed into each other. Leave to dry, then apply wax to protect some areas before adding even richer colours.

Abstract Scarf

you will need
pencil and paper
watercolours or coloured inks
paint palette
artist's paintbrushes
silk pins (push pins)
satin-silk, pre-washed
silk-painting frame
iron-fix (set) silk paints, in 3 colours
large, soft, absorbent paintbrush
batik wax
double boiler or wax pot
household paintbrush
iron
brown craft or lining paper
white spirit (turpentine)
scissors
needle
matching sewing thread

1 Plan your design on paper. It is not necessary to draw it to scale, but it may help to do so. Colour it in, using watercolours or coloured inks, which behave in a similar way to transparent silk paints.

2 Using silk pins (push pins), pin the fabric on to the frame. Check that it is taut and free of wrinkles, and that it will not sag during painting.

3 Mix up the paler silk paint colours first, making sure that you have enough of each colour to cover large areas of the scarf. Use the three base colours to mix additional shades.

4 You will have to work quite quickly if you want the colours to bleed into each other, so place the plan where you can refer to it easily. Paint the paler areas of the scarf, using a large, soft, absorbent paintbrush and light, flowing movements. Leave to dry.

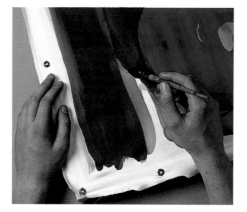

5 Heat the wax in a double boiler or wax pot to a steady 80°C (170°F). Using a household paintbrush, apply the wax to the areas that will remain pale coloured. The wax should be fully absorbed into the cloth and leave the fabric translucent while it is wet. Leave to dry hard.

6 Fill in the darker colours, allowing the colours to bleed and overlap each other to create subtle colour blends. Leave the fabric to dry completely.

7 Unpin the silk from the frame. Remove the wax by ironing it between sheets of brown craft or lining paper. Fix (set) the paints, following the manufacturer's instructions.

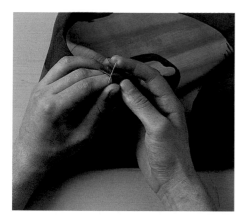

8 Remove any grease marks left on the fabric by soaking it in white spirit (turpentine). Wash the silk several times in warm soapy water to remove the smell. The colours may run slightly, but this will enhance the finished effect. Iron the silk while it is still damp. Trim if necessary so that it is square, then roll the edges and hem stitch by hand.

Simple circles of contrasting colours decorate this unusual ornament, inspired by exquisite Chinese silk kites. It is intended for decorative use, to hang on the wall as you would a picture.

Polka Dot Kite

you will need

silk pins (push pins)

150 x 120cm/60 x 48in silk, pre-washed

silk-painting frame

iron-fix (set) silk paints

fine artist's paintbrushes

paint palette

iron

sewing machine and sewing thread

scissors

fine ribbons, in various colours

needle and pins

tape measure

craft knife

thin bamboo cane

masking tape

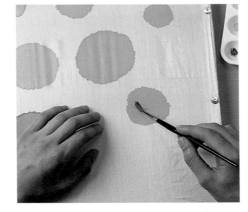

1 Pin the silk to a silk-painting frame, pulling the fabric taut. Load a brush with paint, then paint dots of different colours, spacing them approximately 7.5cm/3in apart. Hold the tip of the brush on the silk, and the colours will bleed outwards. Leave the paints to dry naturally.

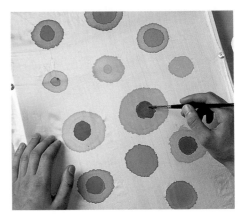

2 Apply a contrast colour dot to the centre of each circle. Allow to dry. Fix (set) the colours with a warm, dry iron. Press and stitch a hem all round. Cut lengths of ribbons and stitch to the corners of the kite.

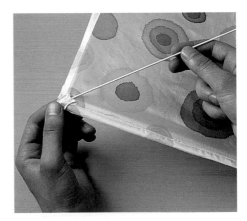

3 For the strut pockets, cut four pieces of silk, 2cm/¾in square, and press under a seam allowance. Pin a square in each corner on the wrong side and stitch around three sides. Measure the length between the diagonal corners and cut two cane struts to fit. Wrap masking tape around the ends, fit them in the pockets and bind with tape where they cross.

Dye a length of crêpe de chine in your chosen colour, then use a fine paintbrush and bleach to remove some of the dye. Wash the bleach out immediately to prevent the fabric from rotting.

Resist-spotted Sarong

you will need

scissors

tape measure

silk crêpe de chine, pre-washed

powder dye

vanishing fabric marker

circular objects, to use as templates

silk pins (push pins)

silk-painting frame

bleach

small bowl

fine artist's paintbrush

needle

matching sewing thread

1 Cut a piece of crêpe de chine 150 x 120cm/60 x 48in. Dampen the fabric and then dye it. Using a vanishing fabric marker, draw a grid on the silk. Draw a circular design on to the fabric, using the grid and circular objects to outline the shapes.

2 Pin the fabric taut on to a frame. Pour a little bleach into a bowl. Using a paintbrush, apply dots of bleach to the design, adding it a little at a time to lighten the fabric. Wash the fabric immediately to remove the bleach and leave to dry.

3 To make a narrow fringe along one short edge, carefully separate and remove horizontal threads using a needle. Finish the other three sides by rolling the edges and hem stitching them neatly in place.

Transform a silk tie with coloured stripes and spots. The stripes are painted with a makeshift painting tool made from a peg (pin) and a cotton wool ball, and the spots are made by adding rock salt to the silk.

Salt-painted Tie

you will need

plain-weave silk tie, white or very pale, pre-washed

transparent gutta and applicator

cotton ball

clothes peg (pin)

iron-fix (set) silk paints, in 2 colours

rock salt

tweezers

medium artist's paintbrush

iron

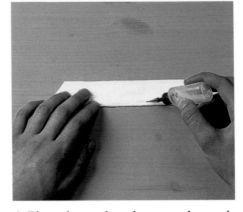

1 Place the tie face down on the work surface. Draw a line with transparent gutta right round the reverse side, about 1cm/½in from the edge. This will prevent the paints from spreading round to the back.

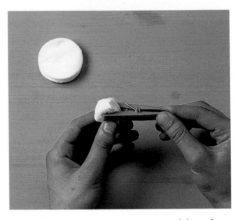

2 Make a large painting tool by clipping a cotton ball into a clothes peg (pin), as shown.

3 Using the first paint colour, apply a stripe of paint across the width of the tie front. While the paint is still damp, place evenly spaced salt crystals along the strip, using tweezers. Continue to apply paint and salt in this way down the length of the tie. When the tie is completely covered, leave it to dry for at least 20 minutes.

4 Using an artist's paintbrush, apply horizontal stripes in the second paint colour between the lines of salt. Leave to dry for 20 minutes.

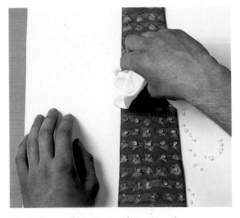

5 When the tie is dry, gently remove the salt crystals. Rock salt comes away quite easily, but smaller salt grains may stick. If this happens, gently rub the tie on itself and the grains will fall away. Iron the tie to fix (set) the paints, following the manufacturer's instructions, then wash it to remove the gutta and press again.

This decorative design is based on a Gothic cathedral window, so rich paint colours are appropriate. Black gutta is used to simulate the effect of the thick leaded lines separating the stained glass.

Stained Glass Panel

you will need

tracing paper and pencil

picture frame

medium-weight silk, pre-washed

masking tape

silk pins (push pins)

silk-painting frame

flat artist's paintbrushes

black gutta

small bowls

iron

iron-fix (set) silk paints, in various

deep colours

thickener

screw-top jar with lid

staple gun

1 Enlarge the template at the back of the book to fit inside the picture frame. Trace it on to the silk, then cover the areas between the lines with masking tape. Using silk pins, pin the silk to a silk-painting frame, pulling the fabric taut.

2 Using a flat artist's paintbrush, fill in the lines between the masking tape with black gutta. Leave the gutta to dry, then apply further coats to make solid lines. Leave to dry. Remove the tape, then take the silk off the frame. Set (fix) the gutta by ironing on the reverse side of the silk.

3 Pin the silk to the painting frame again. Fill in the spaces between the black gutta lines, using coloured silk paints. Leave to dry.

4 In order to paint in more detail, mix thickener into one of the darker colours by placing both in a jar and shaking vigorously. The thickened paint will give a textured brush effect.

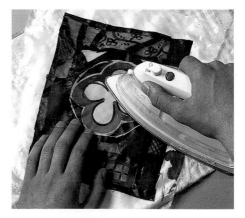

5 Allow the paints to dry, then fix them with an iron, following the manufacturer's instructions. Remove the back from the picture frame. Mount the silk by stretching it over the backless frame, and then secure it at the back using a staple gun.

Decorate a plain silk fan with a lovely floral design in paint and gold gutta. In case adhesive has been used in the manufacture of the fan, add thickener to the paints to prevent them from spreading.

Painted Fan

you will need
pencil
plain silk fan
paper
tracing paper
masking tape
vanishing fabric marker (optional)
gold gutta
gutta applicator fitted with a
fine nib (tip)
thickener
iron-fix (set) silk paints
small bowls
fine artist's paintbrushes

1 Draw around the open fan on to a piece of paper, marking a dotted line where the fabric starts on the fan's handle. Trace the template from the back of the book, and transfer it to paper, within the outline of the fan.

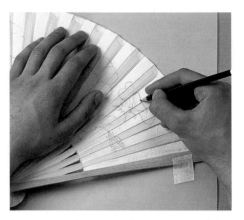

2 Secure the open fan on top of the design with masking tape. Trace the flowers lightly on to the fan, using a soft pencil or vanishing fabric marker. Trace over the design with gold gutta. Leave to dry.

3 The gum used to make the fan may prevent the gutta from acting as a barrier, so mix thickener into the paints to keep them from spreading. Paint the design, using light brushstrokes. To keep the colours clean, use a different brush for each colour. If you need to wash a brush, make sure it is dry before using it again, to prevent the paints becoming too watery.

If you are confident artist, you can draw this lovely design directly on to silk without the aid of a paper pattern or template. Use a ruler and different-sized plates to help you mark out the shapes if not.

Zodiac Scarf

you will need

silk pins (push pins)

silk square, pre-washed and hemmed

silk-painting frame

vanishing fabric marker

paper, tracing paper and

pencil (optional)

transparent gutta and applicator

iron-fix (set) silk paints

fine artist's paintbrushes

iron

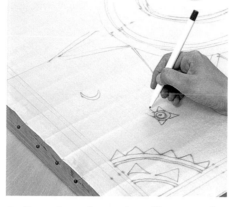

1 Stretch and pin the silk on to the frame. Draw a geometric design on to the silk, using a vanishing fabric marker. Alternatively, draw a design on paper and trace it on to the silk.

2 Apply the gutta over the drawn lines. It is important for the gutta line to be solid, to prevent the paint from bleeding, so check for any gaps. Leave to dry.

3 After the gutta has dried, apply the silk paints. Leave to dry. Carefully remove the silk from the frame and iron to fix (set) the paints, following the manufacturer's instructions. Hand wash to remove the gutta.

Simple flower stencils show up against a background of gently spotted colour, sprayed with a toothbrush. Practise the spraying technique first on paper to get the desired effect.

Patterned Seat Cover

you will need

chair with removable padded seat

paper and pencil

scissors

silk pins (push pins)

silk crêpe de chine, pre-washed

silk-painting frame

vanishing fabric marker

sponge brush

anti-spreading agent

tracing paper

thin cardboard

sticky-backed plastic (contact paper)

iron-fix (set) silk paint

small bowl

old toothbrush

white paper

iron

staple gun

1 Remove the padded seat from the chair, place it on a piece of paper and draw round it. Add a 5cm/2in seam allowance all round and cut out the shape. Pin the crêpe de chine to a silk-painting frame. Place the seat template on top and draw round it with a vanishing fabric marker

2 Using a sponge brush, coat the fabric with anti-spreading agent. Trace the templates from the back of the book, transfer them to thin cardboard and cut out. Place each on sticky-backed plastic (contact paper) and draw around the shapes. Cut out approximately ten of each shape.

3 Peel away the paper backing and stick the shapes on to the fabric to form a pattern. Pour a little paint into a bowl.

4 Dip a toothbrush in paint, and lightly spray it over the fabric. Leave to dry, then peel off the plastic shapes. Sandwich the fabric between sheets of white paper and iron to fix (set) the colour. Hand wash and dry. Stretch it over the seat and attach it to the underside, using a staple gun.

This vibrant picture uses transparent gutta to control the paints. Build up the design by overpainting, using the darkest colours last. Experiment with overpainting your choice of colours before you start.

Poppy Painting

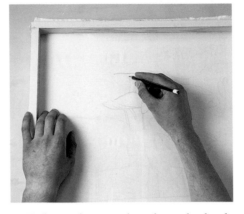

1 Enlarge the template from the back of the book to the size of the finished painting. Pin the silk to the frame and trace the design on to the silk.

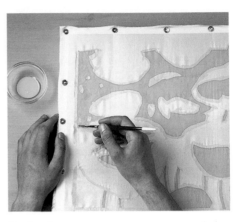

2 Apply transparent gutta around the areas where the palest colours will be. Fill in the palest colour, in this case a yellow which will be over-painted to create shades of green and orange-red. Fix (set) the paint, using an iron. Remove the painting from the frame and rinse away the gutta lines.

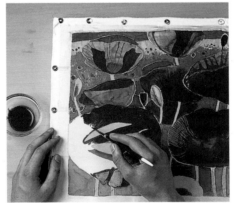

3 Build up the design, keeping the darkest colours until last.

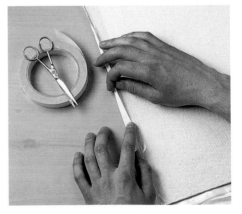

4 Cut a piece of backing to the size of the picture. Put a tiny piece of double-sided tape in each corner of the backing and position the silk on top. Turn the backing over and run double-sided tape along each edge, then pull the fabric round the edge and stick it down. Frame your work.

Make good use of a spare scrap of silk by creating your own handmade card. Use a ready-made greeting card frame with a window cut in it, or mount the silk panels on handmade paper as in the main picture.

Salt-patterned Greetings Card

you will need
silk pins (push pins)
lightweight silk, pre-washed
small silk-painting frame
greetings card frame
soft pencil
iron-fix (set) silk paints
fine artist's paintbrushes
small bowls
rock salt and fine table salt
iron
scissors
spray adhesive (stencil mount)
scrap paper

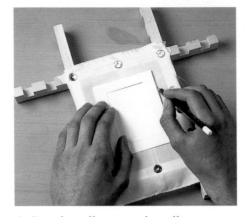

1 Pin the silk on to the silk-painting frame. Place the greetings card frame centrally on the silk and draw round it, using a soft pencil.

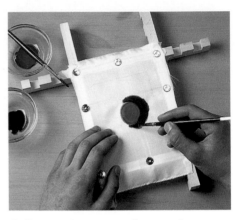

2 Begin to paint an abstract design on the silk within the drawn square. When first learning this technique, it is a good idea to confine your designs to simple spots, stripes, geometric shapes and patterns.

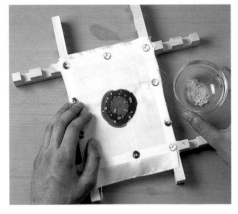

3 While the fabric is still damp with paint but not wet, drop on some rock salt. Build up the design by alternating painting and sprinkling salt. Use different-sized salt crystals, such as rock salt and fine table salt, to create an interesting pattern. Leave to dry completely – this should take about 20 minutes.

4 Remove the silk from the frame and brush the salt from the surface. Fix (set) the paint by pressing with an iron. Open the card and place the frame over the painted silk. Use a soft pencil to draw on the silk along the top and bottom edge of the card, indicating where the folds of the card fall. Close the card and draw the fold lines on the silk.

5 Cut the silk along the lines. Open the card and cover the section to the left of the frame with spray adhesive (stencil mount), protecting the rest of the card with scrap paper. Mount the fabric on the adhesive and trim any excess silk. Lightly spray the back of the frame with adhesive, then fold the card so that the silk is sandwiched in the frame.

Use a very fine silk such as chiffon or georgette for this beautiful, flowing design, which you can make to any size. The thickened paints can be applied with a sponge.

Stencilled Lily Scarf

you will need
tracing paper and pencil
acetate sheet
black marker pen
craft knife and cutting mat
chiffon or georgette, pre-washed
silk pins (push pins)
silk-painting frame
iron-fix (set) silk paints, in 3 colours
wide, soft artist's paintbrush
iron
board and backing cloth
masking tape
tailor's chalk
thickener
screw-top jar with lid
sponge

1 Enlarge the template from the back of the book and trace it on to acetate using a marker pen. Cut around the design and cut out the spots using a craft knife. Stretch and pin the fabric to the frame, pulling it taut as you pin.

2 Apply paint to the fabric in random brushstrokes, allowing each colour to dry before applying the next. Remove from the frame and press the silk. Stretch the silk over a board covered with a cloth and tape down.

3 Position the template and mark each flower with chalk. Mix some thickener with the paint for the flower in a jar. Tape the stencil in place and sponge paint around it. Reposition the stencil and repeat. Leave to dry, then iron to fix the paints.

This spectacular design is painted on silk-satin. The first vibrant colours are allowed to flow into each other and left to dry, then the red petal outlines are added with a fine paintbrush.

Sunflower Cushion Cover

you will need

white silk-satin, 2½ times the size of the cushion pad, plus a 1.5cm/⅝in seam allowance

tailor's chalk

silk pins (push pins)

silk-painting frame

iron-fix (set) silk paints, in yellow, red, blue, turquoise and ultramarine

paint-mixing container

large flat-bristled paintbrush

medium and fine artist's paintbrushes

iron

sewing machine and silk thread

needle

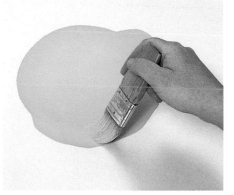

1 Fold the fabric into three panels, two the size of the cushion pad and one half the size (to form the flap). Mark the panels with chalk. Centre the middle panel on the frame. Brush yellow paint from the centre outwards, using a large flat brush.

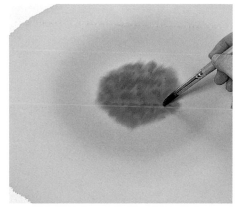

2 Before the paint dries, add red paint to the yellow to make orange and redefine the centre of the circle. Add blue to the paint to make green and make a smaller circle in the centre of the orange. Add dots in the centre with more blue paint. Leave to dry.

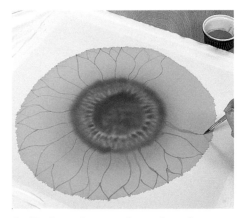

3 Define the petals with red paint. Fill in the background with shades of blue. Fix the paint. Press under and stitch a double hem on each short edge. Fold right sides together, so that the flap covers half the front. Fold the back over both, then stitch the side seams. Turn through, insert a cushion pad and stitch the gap.

Paint stripes of colour, then spoon on lines of salt while the silk is still damp to create a soft, watery effect. Alternate the painting and the salt, rather than painting the whole area first.

Abstract Picture Frame

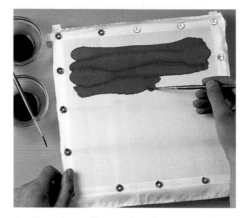

1 Pin the silk to the frame, pulling the fabric taut. Paint a few stripes of alternate colours, making the stripes at least 2.5cm/1in wide.

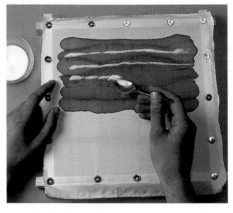

2 While the silk is damp, spoon lines of salt grains along the stripes. Continue alternating paint and salt until the surface is covered. Leave to dry. Brush off the salt, remove the silk from the frame and iron to fix (set) the paints.

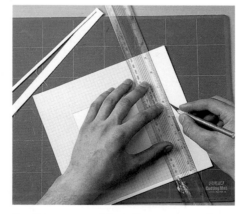

3 Cut out a 20cm/8in square from graph paper. Draw a 10cm/4in square centrally within it and cut out. Glue the paper to mounting board and cut out with a craft knife.

4 Centre the frame on a 25cm/10in square of wadding (batting). Trim off the corners of the wadding, then fold and stick the surplus down with adhesive tape. Cut an "x" across the central square of wadding, trim to 2cm/¾in, turn back over the frame edges and tape down.

5 Pin the silk with the wrong side of the silk against the wadding. Trim the excess silk to 3cm/1¼in. Cut an "x" in the silk inside the frame and trim to 3cm/1¼in. Fold the outer corners over the back, fold the flaps in and stitch.

6 Wrap the silk edges over the frame and lace them together with long stitches. Do not pull the silk too tightly or the shape will distort. Stitch a small ribbon rose to each inside corner of the frame.

7 Cut a 20cm/8in square of mounting board to make the backing. Cut a tall, right-angled triangle, score along the longest side 1cm/½in from the edge and bend it over to make a stand. Trim the bottom edge and check the board will stand properly. Glue the stand to the backing, starting from the bottom edge. Attach the backing to the frame by gluing along three sides, leaving one side free so that a picture can be slipped inside. To make the picture permanent, add the picture before gluing all four sides and attaching the backing. Leave the glue to dry.

An abstract geometric design makes a highly unusual clock, with a ready-made clock movement and hands attached in the centre. Heavy habotai silk is ideal for this project.

Silk Clock Face

you will need

heavyweight habotai silk, pre-washed

silk-painting frame

silk pins (push pins)

black felt-tipped pen

tracing paper

masking tape

vanishing fabric marker

metallic gutta and applicator

iron-fix (set) silk paints

palette

paintbrushes

white paper

iron

scissors

heavy cardboard

rubber-based glue

fine braid

clock movement and hands

1 Stretch the silk on to the frame and pin in position. The fabric must be absolutely taut. Trace the template at the back of the book, in felt-tipped pen, allowing for a generous border all around the design.

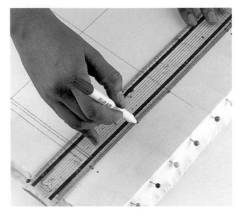

2 Secure the tracing paper underneath the silk frame with pieces of masking tape at each corner. Turn the silk frame over and draw on to the silk with the vanishing fabric marker, going over the design below.

3 Apply the metallic gutta over the outline of the design, then leave to dry thoroughly.

4 Apply the silk paints, taking care not to splash or go over any lines of gutta. Paint in the design. Leave the fabric to dry before removing it from the frame.

5 Place the painted silk between two sheets of clean white paper and iron it, according to the manufacturer's instructions, to fix (set) the paint. To assemble the clock, cut two pieces of cardboard to the size of the finished design. Glue them together to form the base for the silk and leave under a heavy object to dry for 24 hours.

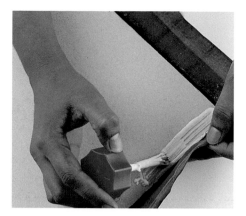

7 Cut a piece of silk slightly smaller than the block and stick it on to the back of the block to cover the joins and neaten the edges. Trim the edges with fine braid.

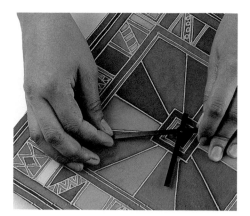

6 Trim the edges of the silk slightly larger than the cardboard. Centre the cardboard block on the silk and glue in place, stretching the silk to fit.

8 Make a hole in the centre of the design and attach the clock movement and hands.

Hang this silk fabric where it will move gently in the softest breeze. The stylized motifs, drawn freehand, are based on Indian Mogul architectural features such as doors and arched windows.

Double-panelled Room Divider

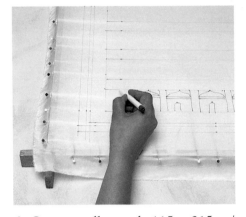

1 Cut two silk panels 115 x 215cm/ 45 x 85in. Stretch the first over the frame, using silk pins. Using a ruler and vanishing fabric marker, draw the borders on the silk, then add the individual motifs. Draw your design on paper first for reference, if you wish.

2 Draw over the lines of the design with gold gutta. Turn over the screen to make sure that the gutta has penetrated through the silk. If there are gaps in the lines, add more gutta to the back of the fabric. Leave to dry.

3 Mix the paint colours, ensuring that you have enough of each. Fill in the solid areas of the design, using artist's paintbrushes. If you dot a little paint in the centre of each area, it will quickly spread as far as the gutta lines.

4 Using a paintbrush, apply diluted washes of colour to fill in the background and borders. Allow to dry and unpin the silk from the frame. Iron to fix (set) the colours. Repeat with the second panel. Stitch the panels together. Pin and slip stitch gold cord around the edge. Stitch the three gold tassels to the bottom corners.

This beautiful painted and embroidered shawl was inspired by the Indian custom in which a bride's palms are hennaed with intricate designs the night before her wedding.

Indian Motif Shawl

you will need

large heatproof bowl

tablespoon and teaspoon

salt

2 teabags

1m/1yd of 90cm/36in-wide habotai silk, pre-washed

iron

tracing paper and pencil

masking tape

vanishing fabric marker

silk-painting frame

small hammer

dressmaker's pins

gutta applicator

gutta

iron-fix (set) silk paints

palette

medium artist's paintbrush

white paper

embroidery hoop

sewing machine, with a darning foot

machine embroidery threads, in various colours

scissors

needle

1 Fill a bowl with boiling water. Dissolve 60ml/4 tbsp of salt and immerse two teabags in the water. Remove the teabags, then immerse the silk for 10 minutes. Rinse and press the silk using a cool iron.

3 Stretch the fabric over the wooden frame, using a hammer and pins. Ensure that the fabric is taut and that it has no wrinkles. Fill the dispenser with gutta and apply it along the lines of the design. Allow to dry.

5 Leave the paint to dry, then brush away the salt grains. Remove the silk from the frame and place it between two sheets of white paper. Fix (set) the paints, by pressing the silk with an iron following the manufacturer's instructions. Wash the fabric to remove the gutta. Draw star motifs freehand on the background fabric with the fabric marker.

2 Trace the hand template, enlarging as required. Stretch the silk over the template and tape it down. Trace with a vanishing fabric marker. Repeat the design by drawing a grid and rotating the design 90° each time.

4 Pour the silk paints into the palette compartments. Dot a little paint into the centre of each area to be coloured. Apply a wash of colour to the palm then, while the paint is still wet, drop 5ml/1 tsp of salt into the centre.

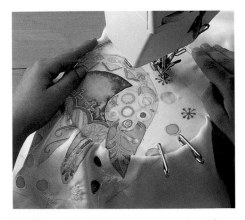

6 Place the fabric in an embroidery hoop and machine embroider the stars in coloured threads.

7 Using the fabric marker, draw additional circles to overlap the painted ones. Fill in the circles with matching embroidery, working a spiral from the centre to the outline. Stitch two or three lines around the palm area, working small bobbles at intervals. Cut away the excess fabric to within 5cm/2in of the design edge.

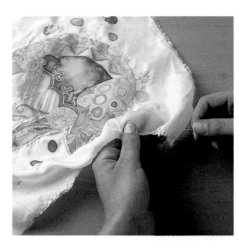

8 Using a needle, carefully pull away the threads around the raw edges to make a fringe.

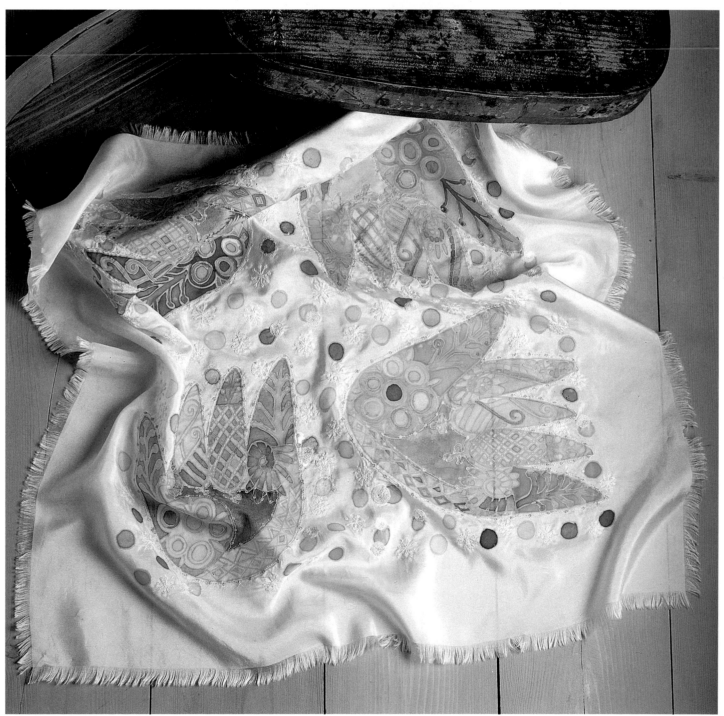

Batik

Traditional batik is known for its delicate patterns of vein-like lines, created by applying hot wax to the surface of the fabric and then cracking the wax when it is cold so that coloured dyes can seep in. The technique of wax resist can be used to create designs large and small, including napkins, room dividers and beautiful silk and velvet scarves.

Wax, Crackle and Paint

Traditional batik dyeing has a very long history, dating back over 2,000 years. The word "batik" is Indonesian, and batik is most commonly associated with the Indonesian island of Java.

The batik technique works on the principle that wax acts as a barrier, or "resist", to water and therefore also to diluted dyes.

The wax has to be heated to the correct temperature before being applied to the fabric surface, and it is important to maintain a constant temperature, so a thermometer is essential. The wax should make the fabric semi-transparent when it is applied; if the fabric remains opaque, the wax isn't hot enough. If in doubt, test a spare piece of fabric before embarking on the final piece.

Various brushes and tools (even a piece of string) can be used to apply the

wax, but the traditional Indonesian "tjanting" allows very precise and delicate patterns to be drawn in the same way as a pen. It takes a little practice to master the flow of the hot wax through the tjanting so that it comes out evenly in a

continuous, unbroken line. As the wax cools, it becomes brittle and can be gently cracked by rubbing the fabric between your hands. When the waxed fabric is immersed in a dye bath the colour seeps into the cracks, creating a random, unpredictable and unique colour pattern. The more cracks you make, the more the dye will penetrate the fabric. Further layers of wax and dye can be

applied to the cleaned fabric to build up a complex design, although striking, contemporary effects can be achieved quite simply using just one or two vibrant colours.

In a quite different version of batik – known as the direct dyeing method and as "false batik", the fabric is not dyed in a dye

bath but is painted using iron-fix (set) silk paints or fabric paints.

Whichever method you choose, traditional and modern batik designs work very successfully on a wide range of smooth, natural fabrics, including cotton, silk and even leather.

The most important materials used in batik are the wax for the resist, the double boiler to heat the wax, and the dyes or paints to colour the fabric, depending on which technique you are using.

Materials

wax and dyes to penetrate the fibres. Cotton can be boiled, but silk should be dry-cleaned to remove the wax.

General-purpose batik wax

Available ready-mixed in granular form from craft suppliers, this is the simplest wax for a beginner to use. Different waxes are available to create special effects. Heat and apply the wax following the manufacturer's instructions. Work in a well ventilated area.

Kitchen paper

Use to blot up excess paint.

Leather

Batik works well on leather, using a clear, water-soluble household glue or gum instead of wax as a resist. Don't use wax on leather as it will stain it. Special dyes and finishing treatments such as leather lacquer spray are available for leather – always follow the manufacturer's instructions.

Newspaper, brown craft or lining paper

Insert waxed fabric between sheets of paper and iron to remove the wax. Replace with new paper until all the wax is removed.

Sponge

Use to make stencils.

Bleach

Colour can be removed from a pre-dyed fabric by placing it in a bowl of diluted bleach. Always wear rubber gloves and work in a well-ventilated area. Rinse fabric with water and vinegar to neutralize the bleach.

Cotton wool (Cotton balls)

Clip a wad of cotton wool into a clothes peg (pin) to make a homemade painting tool for covering large areas.

Dyes and silk paints

Use cold-water dyes, in powder or liquid form. Dyes or silk paints can also be applied to fabric in concentrated form. Special dyes are available for working with leather.

Fabrics

Use natural fabrics such as cotton and silk – those without texture are the most suitable. Pre-wash the fabric to remove any dressing, and to allow the

Heating wax for batik requires a wax pot or double boiler, and a thermometer. You will probably also use a dye bath or painting frame, and a traditional tjanting.

Equipment

Chalk
Can be used to lightly trace a design on to dark-coloured fabric.

Craft knife
Use to cut thick paper and cardboard. Work on a cutting mat to protect the work surface.

Dye bath, buckets and bowls
Special shallow dye baths are ideal for batik dyeing. Alternatively, use a metal or plastic catering tray, or a large saucepan, bucket or bowl in which the fabric can move freely. If you are using a hot-water dye, the dye bath must be heatproof. Keep the fabric immersed so that the dye penetrates evenly.

Hairdryer and iron
Use a hairdryer to fix (set) silk dyes that are awkward shapes. Be careful not to melt the wax. Use an iron to remove wax from fabric and to set dye.

Masking tape
Use to attach fabric to a board or work surface to hold it in place.

Paintbrushes
Artist's and decorator's paintbrushes of various sizes can be used. Use a separate brush to apply wax. Use sponge brushes to apply paint over large areas of fabric. Alternatively, use a large kitchen sponge.

Painting frame
Stretch fabric taut over a wooden painting frame before tracing a design on to the fabric surface.

Rubber gloves
Wear rubber gloves when dyeing fabric to avoid staining your hands.

Thermometer
Some wax pots are thermostatically controlled, but, if not, a kitchen thermometer is essential to keep the batik wax at a constant temperature while you are applying it to the fabric.

Tjanting
This traditional pen-like tool is used to draw wax designs on the fabric. Available with many size nibs (tips).

Wool dauber
A tool used to apply leather dyes.

Good preparation is the key to success with every fabric painting technique, and will help to ensure that better and more consistent results are achieved.

Techniques

Making a basic wooden painting frame

A wooden frame is essential for batik. Make a basic frame slightly larger than the size of the finished batik piece.

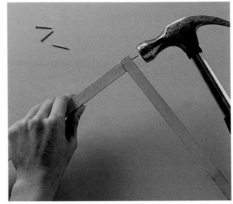

1 Cut four pieces of planed wood to the size you want your frame to be. Using wood adhesive, glue two sets of two pieces together to make right angles. Allow the glue to set.

2 Tap one or two panel pins (tacks) into the corner joint to hold it firmly. Glue the right angles together to make the frame and nail the corners as before.

3 Sand down any rough pieces of wood so that it is free of splinters. Protect the frame from dye by covering it with masking tape.

Pinning fabric over the frame

Special assa pins (push pins) with three prongs are available from craft suppliers, for fixing fabric to the wooden frame.

1 Cut a piece of cloth to the size of the frame and place the first assa pin (push pin) in the centre of the furthest edge.

2 Working out towards each corner, continue placing the pins an equal distance apart. Pull the fabric taut.

3 Pull the fabric across the frame, and place the pins opposite to those on the first side. Pull the fabric taut. Repeat on the other two sides.

Traditional batik

Traditional batik is best used when large areas of colour are required. When using a dye bath, use a cold-water dye so the consistency of the wax is not affected, and keep the cloth flat while submerged in dye.

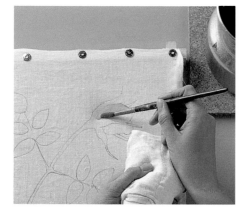

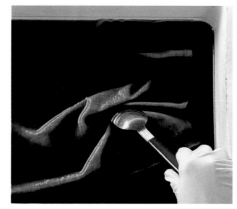

1 Place the batik wax in a wax pot or double boiler and gently heat it to a steady 80°C (170°F). Apply melted wax along the outline of the design, using a tjanting or other instrument such as a paintbrush or cotton wool. The wax should leave a transparent line on the fabric. If the wax is not hot enough, it will sit on the surface of the fabric without penetrating the fibres sufficiently. Leave the wax to dry.

2 Mix up a dye bath with a cold water dye, following the dye manufacturer's instructions. Remove the cloth from the frame. Dampen it and place it in the dye bath, keeping the waxed area as flat as possible. When the desired colour has been achieved, remove the fabric from the bath and rinse it in cold water. Unless cracking is required, be careful not to crease the fabric while rinsing. Hang it up to dry.

3 When the cloth is dry, re-pin it on to the frame, pulling it taut, and fill in any areas with wax that you want to remain the colour of the first dye. Check the back to make sure that the wax has penetrated sufficiently. Prepare a second dye bath. Add the fabric to it, being careful not to fold the waxed areas. After dyeing, rinse it thoroughly in cold water. Hang up to dry through.

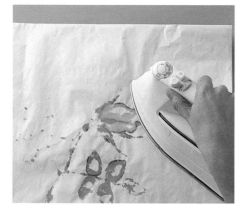

4 Remove the wax by ironing the cloth between pieces of newspaper, brown paper or lining paper.

5 Wax and dye can be added to build up more layers of colour and detail. However, most dyes can only be overlaid about three times.

False method or direct dyeing

This principle uses wax as a boundary, where one colour is separated from another by a line of wax. It is imperative that the lines of wax have no breaks, or the colours will bleed into each other.

1 Pin the fabric to the frame, transfer the design and heat the wax as for the traditional batik method. Using a tjanting, draw in any outlines with wax. When the wax is applied, the fabric should become semi-transparent. If the wax has not penetrated the fibres sufficiently, the fabric will remain opaque. Check for breaks in the wax outline and fill them in by waxing on the back.

2 Using fabric dye (transparent dyes not containing binders, such as silk paints, are ideal), fill in the required areas with a paintbrush. Work quickly to ensure an even colour. If you choose to use a thick fabric paint, be sure to dilute it to the consistency of ink.

3 Draw in more of the outline with molten wax and tjanting. Check the back of the fabric again to make sure that the wax has penetrated the fibres of the fabric sufficiently.

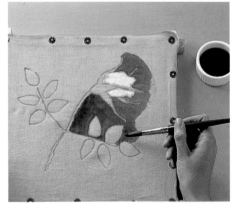

4 Using a different colour, fill in the background with a paintbrush. Further applications of dye can be made on the remaining non-waxed areas.

5 Apply a third colour. Waxing and dyeing can continue indefinitely or until the whole cloth is covered. To remove the wax, see Finishing.

Special treatments   Although the tjanting is the traditional tool used for applying wax, other tools such as paintbrushes and cotton wool pads can be used to achieve different effects. Once complete, take time to finish the work methodically.

Tjanting

The tjanting allows delicate designs to be drawn on to fabric with wax. Keep movements light and do not press on the fabric too hard as this may block the flow of wax.

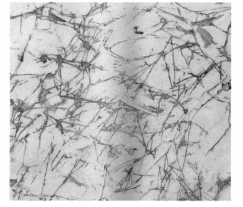

Cracking

Here the fabric was coated in a layer of wax. It was crumpled, to crack the wax surface. Dye the fabric in a dye bath for best results and use a brittle crackle wax.

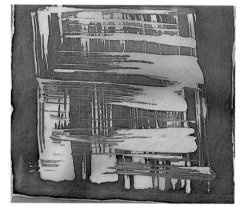

Decorator's paintbrush

This cross-hatching effect was made using a medium-sized decorator's paintbrush. Lightly draw the waxed brush across the undyed fabric horizontally and then vertically.

Finishing   Wax must be removed from the finished batik to restore the fabric's drape. Ironing will remove most of the wax, but it will be necessary to boil or dry-clean the fabric to remove final marks and wax residue.

1 Break away as much of the hardened wax as you can. Do not scrub the fabric as this may damage the surface.

2 Place the batik between sheets of newspaper, brown or lining paper, and iron until the wax is absorbed. Repeat until wax is no longer being absorbed.

3 To use the boiling method, break off as much wax as possible then place the fabric in boiling water for about 10 minutes, stirring continuously.

This intricate batik design uses four different dye baths to build up the layers of colour. Chrome yellow, turquoise, peacock blue and navy make a stunning combination.

Abstract Cushion Cover

you will need

82cm/32in of 90cm/36in-wide white cotton fabric, pre-washed

scissors

ruler

paper

black felt-tipped pen

pencil

general-purpose wax

wax pot or double boiler

adjustable tapestry frame

drawing (push) pins

tjanting

paper towels

old artist's paintbrush

bucket

salt

rubber gloves

urea and soda (sodium carbonate)

dyes, in chrome yellow, turquoise, peacock blue and navy

newspaper, old sheet or cover

iron

needle

matching sewing thread

sewing machine (optional)

dressmaker's pins

Velcro

square cushion pad to fit

1 Cut one 47cm/18½in square and two 47 x 30cm/18½ x 12in rectangles of fabric. Enlarge the template from the back of the book on to a 41cm/16in square of paper and go over the lines with a felt-tipped pen. Trace the design on to the centre of the square.

3 For larger areas of the design, carefully outline them with the tjanting first, then fill them in using an old artist's paintbrush. Once all the white areas have been waxed, turn the frame over and, if necessary, re-wax any areas the wax has not penetrated completely. Leave to dry thoroughly.

2 Heat the wax in a wax pot or double boiler. Stretch the fabric square on to the tapestry frame and secure with drawing (push) pins. Use a tjanting to wax the areas you want to remain white. Use a pad of paper towels to prevent drips.

4 Prepare a yellow dye bath. Half fill a bucket with cold water, dissolve 30ml/2 tbsp of urea in 600ml/1 pint of lukewarm water. In a separate container mix 5ml/1 tsp of chrome yellow dye to a paste. Stir the urea solution into the dye paste and pour into the bucket. Dissolve 60ml/4 tbsp salt in 600ml/1 pint/2½ cups of lukewarm water and add to the bucket. Add the batik square and the rectangles, and stir for 6 minutes. Dissolve 15ml/1 tbsp of soda/sodium carbonate in a little warm water and add to the bucket. Leave the fabric to soak for 45 minutes, stirring occasionally. Remove and rinse in cold water until the water runs clear. Hang the fabric out to dry.

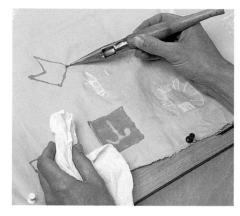

5 Apply wax to the areas that are to stay yellow.

6 Prepare a turquoise dye bath in the same way and immerse the fabric for 45 minutes. Rinse and dry it, then apply wax to the areas that are to remain green.

7 Prepare a blue dye bath with 10ml/ 2 tsp of dye, and leave the fabric in it for 1 hour. Rinse and dry the fabric, then wax the areas that are to remain blue. Plunge the fabric into cold water to crack the large areas of wax. Prepare another dye bath using 15ml/1 tbsp of navy dye. Leave the fabric to soak for several hours, then rinse and leave to dry.

8 Protect your ironing board with an old sheet. Place the batik between several layers of paper and iron over it to melt the wax. Keep replacing the newspaper until most of the wax has been removed. The last traces of wax can be removed by dry-cleaning or by immersing the fabric in boiling water. Press all the pieces while they are still damp.

9 Stitch a small hem along the long edge of each rectangle of fabric. Overlap the hems to make a 47cm/ 18½in square, right sides facing up, then pin and tack (baste) together.

10 With right sides together, pin the front and back of the cover together. Stitch around the outside edge of the batik. Trim the seams, clip the corners and turn right side out.

11 Remove the tacking threads. Ease out the corners and press the seams. Pin and stitch close to the inside edge of the border, and trim the threads. Sew a small piece of Velcro to the opening edges of the cover. Insert the cushion pad and close the Velcro.

Paint the background to this simple design using a homemade tool consisting of a cotton ball clipped into a clothes peg (pin). Scrunching the batik wax creates the distinctive vein-like batik lines.

Crackled Scarf

you will need

tracing paper and pencil

paper

silk pins (push pins)

lightweight silk, pre-washed

silk-painting frame

cotton balls

clothes pegs (pins)

iron-fix (set) silk paints

small bowls

medium and large artist's paintbrushes

batik wax

double boiler or wax pot

brown craft or lining paper

absorbent cloth or paper

iron

white spirit (turpentine) (optional)

needle

matching sewing thread

sewing machine (optional)

1 Trace the template at the back of the book on to paper. Pin the silk to a silk-painting frame and place it upside down over the design. Using a soft pencil, trace the design on to the back of the silk. This will reverse the design; if you want it to be the original way round, transfer it first on to tracing paper.

2 Make a large painting tool for each colour by clipping a cotton ball into a clothes peg (pin). Paint the base colours, which should be the palest in the design, on to the silk, allowing each one to dry before applying the next colour.

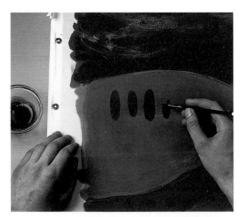

3 Using a medium artist's paintbrush, overpaint small areas of the pale base colours in a darker colour to start building up the design. Leave to dry.

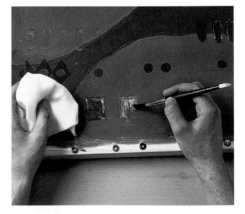

4 Heat the wax in a wax pot or double boiler (see Techniques). Use a large artist's paintbrush to cover the central area of the silk with solid wax. Add details with the medium paintbrush. Leave to cool.

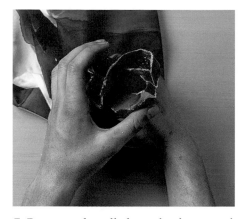

5 Remove the silk from the frame and scrunch the central waxed area to crack the surface. Replace the silk on the frame.

6 Using the large paintbrush, paint over the entire piece with the darkest colour, ensuring that it sinks into the cracks. Leave to dry.

7 Remove the fabric from the frame, place it between sheets of brown craft or lining paper, on top of an absorbent cloth or paper, and iron out the wax. Fix (set) the silk paints, following the manufacturer's instructions. Remove any remaining grease marks by soaking the fabric in white spirit (turpentine), then hand wash it in soapy water to remove the smell. Stitch a hem along the scarf edges.

Leather may seem an unusual material for batik, but you can crumple it in the same way as fabric to create the distinctive "cracked" effect. Use gum instead of wax, and special leather dyes.

Leather Book Cover

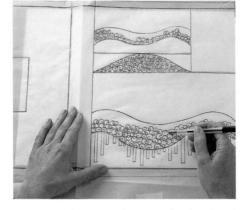

1 Trace the template at the back of the book. Dampen the leather with cotton wool (cotton balls), then transfer the design from the paper on to the leather. Cut out the leather for the book cover, using a craft knife and cutting mat. Leave the leather to dry. Brush the gum over the leather on the areas that will remain neutral.

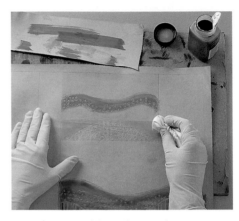

2 Wearing rubber gloves, dip a cotton wool pad or a wool dauber, into the green dye. Press the pad on to a scrap of leather to remove any excess dye. Beginning in one corner, gently move the pad over the leather surface. Leave to dry naturally. Apply gum to those areas that will remain green. Repeat with the yellow dye.

3 Leave the green dye to dry naturally, and coat with gum in the same way. In turn, apply red dye to the leather with a cotton wool pad. When completely dry, block out with gum those areas that are to remain red or green.

4 Add the black in the same way. Crumple the leather to achieve a good "cracked" effect on the surface. Place the leather on a board and remove the gum with a large piece of damp cotton wool. Wash thoroughly with plenty of cold water.

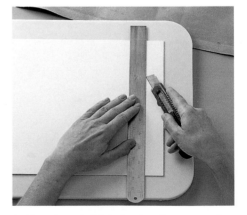

5 Bend and fold the leather into the desired shape while it is still damp. Mitre the corners. Leave to dry. Spray adhesive (stencil mount) on to the reverse side. Place a piece of mount board over the top and press the pieces together. Spray with lacquer.

This colourful abstract on black cotton was inspired by the artworks of Joan Miró. Test the cotton first to check that it is bleachable. Some of the wax remains in the fabric to keep it slightly stiff.

Modern Painting

you will need

tracing paper and pencil

thin paper

black pen

silk pins (push pins)

65 x 45cm/26 x 18in piece black cotton (bleachable), pre-washed

65 x 45cm/26 x 18in painting frame

masking tape

chalk

general-purpose wax

wax pot or double boiler

medium decorator's paintbrush

rubber gloves

bowls

bleach

vinegar

dye brush

dyes, in red, yellow, orange, blue and green

iron

newspaper, brown or lining paper

sewing machine

black sewing thread

2 pieces of 1cm/⅜in dowelling, 50cm/20in long

fishing wire or string

1 Trace the template to the required size on to thin paper using a black pen. Pin the fabric to the frame, then tape the design on the back of the fabric. Hold the frame up to a light source and lightly trace the design on the front of the fabric, using chalk.

2 Heat the wax in a wax pot or double boiler (see Techniques). Apply it with a medium decorator's paintbrush to the areas that will remain black. Check that the wax has penetrated to the back of the fabric. If necessary, wax the same area from the back.

3 Remove the fabric from the frame. Wearing rubber gloves and working in a ventilated area, place the fabric in a bowl of thin bleach. Leave the fabric until it has turned cream, agitating it to allow even bleaching. Rinse in water, then rinse in water with a splash of vinegar to neutralize the bleach. Rinse in water again.

4 Pin the fabric back on the frame and leave it to dry. Check that the waxed lines are solid and re-wax any lines that are cracked. Using a dye brush, paint the dyes in the non-waxed areas, following the manufacturer's instructions. Leave to dry.

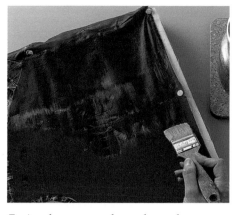

7 Hem both sides of the picture. Stitch a 2cm/¾in hem at the top and bottom. Insert a piece of dowelling at both ends. Attach a piece of fishing wire or string to both ends of the top piece of dowelling for hanging.

5 Apply wax to the coloured areas so that all the fabric is covered in wax. This is to avoid a wax shadow on the final picture. Remove the fabric from the frame.

6 Iron the fabric between sheets of newspaper, brown or lining paper. Continue ironing, replacing the paper until no more wax appears through. The cloth will remain slightly stiff.

Use simple sponge shapes to create an alternating design of evenly spaced circles and stars on this lovely sarong. Areas of plain colour make an effective contrast to the batik.

Cotton Sarong

you will need
tracing paper and pencil
scissors
masking tape
sponge
felt-tipped pen
craft knife
150cm/60in of 90cm/36in-wide
thin cotton, pre-washed
plastic board or surface
general-purpose wax
wax pot or double boiler
large decorator's brush
large bowls
rubber gloves
dyes, in yellow and dark green
iron
newspaper, brown or lining paper
sewing machine
matching sewing thread

1 Trace the templates at the back of the book. Cut them out and attach to a sponge, using masking tape. Draw around each template. With a craft knife, cut out the sponge shapes.

2 Pin one end of the cotton fabric on to a plastic board. Heat the wax in a wax pot or double boiler (see Techniques) and apply with a large brush around the edge of the sarong.

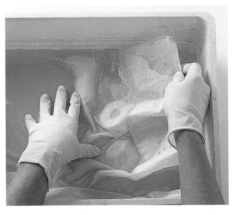

3 Using the circular sponge, apply the wax, leaving approximately 8cm/3in between each circle. Repeat the pattern around the edge of the border.

4 Wet the fabric thoroughly. Dye the wet fabric yellow, following the manufacturer's instructions. Hang it up to dry. Pin the fabric back on to the plastic board. Using the same brush, re-wax the border to keep the yellow crackle effect. Wax over the circles again, using the same sponge stencil. Using the cross stencil, apply the wax between the circles.

5 Put the fabric in a bowl of water, then dye the wet fabric dark green, following the manufacturer's instructions. Hang it up to dry.

6 Iron the fabric between sheets of paper, until no more wax appears through the paper. Dry-clean the fabric to remove the excess wax. Turn in the raw edges and stitch in place.

Batik on silk velvet creates a lovely mottled effect. Use a sponge to help the wax penetrate the thick pile of the velvet, and apply at least two layers of wax over each area to protect the fabric.

Silk Velvet Scarf

you will need

tracing paper and pencil

scissors

felt-tipped pen

sponge

craft knife

silk pins (push pins) or masking tape

130 x 27cm/52 x 10½in of white silk velvet

plastic board or surface

general-purpose wax

wax pot or double boiler

large bowls

rubber gloves

bucket

dyes, in gold and dark brown

newspaper

iron

brown or lining paper (optional)

knife

sewing machine

matching sewing thread

needle

1 Trace the diamond template at the back of the book. Cut it out and draw around it on to a piece of sponge. Cut out the shape with a craft knife.

2 Pin or tape one end of the silk velvet on to a plastic board or surface.

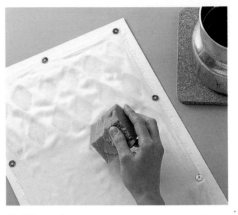

3 Heat the wax in a wax pot or double boiler (see Techniques). Apply it in three rows, using the diamond-shaped sponge stencil. Apply single diamonds randomly along the scarf length. Reattach the scarf at the other end and repeat the design. Repeat the process to protect the velvet. Unpin the fabric.

4 Place the velvet in a bowl of water. Wearing rubber gloves, put the wet fabric in a bucket of gold dye, agitate and remove after approximately 3 minutes. Blot between sheets of newspaper to remove excess dye, then hang up to dry.

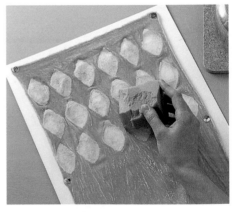

5 Pin the fabric to the plastic board. Wax the gold areas using the sponge stencil, then repeat the waxing to protect the gold velvet. Roughly wax over the white diamonds again, to keep the gold crackle effect. Remove the fabric from the board.

◄ **6** Wet the fabric, then dye it dark brown and agitate for a few minutes. Blot between sheets of paper and hang up to dry. Iron the velvet between sheets of newsprint, pile side down. When the wax is softened, scrape it off the pile with a knife. Turn the velvet over again and keep ironing until most of the wax has been absorbed by the paper. Remove the excess wax by dry cleaning. Stitch the fabric together lengthwise, with right sides facing. Leave an 8cm/3in-gap along the side and turn the scarf right side out. Hand sew the gap. Steam the seams flat.

The marbled effect on this cotton fabric was created using the "crack-le" technique. Some of the wax is deliberately left in the fabric to make it water-resistant, and the bag also has a practical nylon lining.

Crackle-finish Cosmetic Bag

1 Cut a piece of cotton fabric the size required for the finished washbag, adding 1cm/½in seam allowance all round. Using silk pins (push pins), pin the fabric on to a wooden painting frame. Heat the wax in a wax pot or double boiler (see Techniques), then cover the entire fabric with wax using a medium decorator's paintbrush.

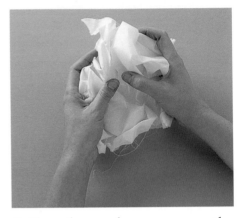

2 Once the wax has set, remove the fabric from the frame and crumple it firmly between both hands. Small cracks should appear in the surface of the wax. Once the fabric has been "cracked" enough, smooth it out flat and dampen.

3 Prepare a navy blue dye bath, following the manufacturer's instructions. Place the damp fabric in the bath for the recommended time, allowing the dye to penetrate the cracks in the wax.

4 Rinse the fabric in cold water until the water runs clear. Leave to dry. Re-pin the fabric on to the painting frame. Heat the wax with a hairdryer until it melts, so that the molten wax seals up the cracks.

5 When the wax has set, crumple the fabric again between your hands. Repeat step 3, using a strong green dye. Rinse the batik until the water runs clear, then remove as much wax as possible with your fingers.

6 Iron out more of the wax by placing the batik between pieces of newspaper, brown or lining paper. Keep renewing the paper and ironing until the fabric has regained most of its flexibility, but still contains some wax.

7 Cut the batik in half then cut two pieces of nylon fabric to the same sizes, for the lining. With right sides together, pin, then machine stitch up one side of the batik, leaving a 1cm/½in gap 1cm/½in from the top. Iron the side seam flat, then oversew around the gap by hand to reinforce it. Stitch the other side seam and across the bottom to make the bag.

8 Take the two pieces of lining and stitch round three sides, using a 1cm/½in seam allowance, to make another bag. Place the batik bag inside the lining bag, with wrong sides together.

9 Open up a piece of bias binding long enough to fit the length of the top of the bag. Align the raw edge of the bag with one long edge of the binding. Pin, then stitch round the edge of the bag, using the crease on the bias binding as a guide for stitching. Turn the bag right side out. Fold the bias binding over to the right side of the bag, and fold the raw edge in. Top stitch the binding to the bag, keeping as close to the folded edge of the binding as possible.

10 Stitch two parallel lines to make a channel round the top of the bag just clearing the top and bottom of the gap in the side seam.

11 Thread ribbon or cord through the hole and along the channel. Pull up to close the bag.

Transform an old canvas deckchair with this wonderfully eye-catching design. Allowing the colours to bleed into each other creates the soft, furry effect of the tiger's mane and stripes.

Tiger Deckchair

you will need

old deckchair

tracing paper and pencil

heavyweight canvas, pre-washed

painting frame

assa (push) pins

tjanting

general-purpose wax

wax pot or double boiler

brushes (for wax)

dyes (for direct dyeing method)

soft brushes (for dye)

large sponge brush or soft

kitchen sponge

hairdryer (optional)

newspaper, brown or lining paper

iron

scissors

dressmaker's pins

sewing machine

matching sewing thread

hammer

upholstery pins

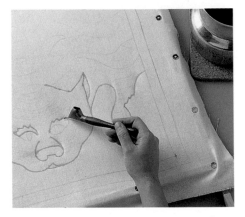

1 Remove the fabric from the deckchair. Draw around it adding 2cm/¾in all round for seams. Trace the design provided on to the canvas. Continue the stripes until the cloth is covered. Pin the cloth taut to a frame.

2 Heat the wax in a wax pot or double boiler. Using a tjanting, wax the outline of the tiger's head, paws, eyebrows and irises. If the wax does not penetrate the heavy fabric, so fill in the breaks in the wax on the back.

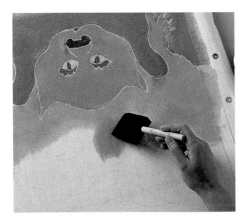

3 Using a tjanting and/or brush, block in the claws and whites of the eyes with wax. Fill in the iris and eyebrows with dark brown and olive green dyes. Using a larger brush, fill in the background to the tiger (the base of the cloth on the finished chair).

4 Fill in the tiger background colour. Fade the colours from a pale orange at the tiger's head to a strong cherry red at the other end of the fabric. Work quickly so that the colours bleed into each other while still wet. To help with quick coverage, use a large sponge brush or soft kitchen sponge.

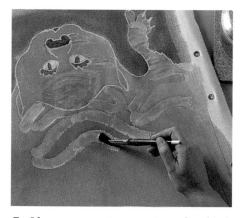 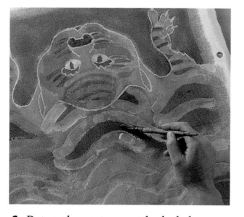 

5 If you are using an iron-fix (set) dye, use a hairdryer to help dry the fabric. When the fabric is dry, use a brush to wax the outline to the tiger stripes. Use a thicker brush when you are about halfway down the fabric.

6 Paint the stripes with dark brown. Remove the batik from the frame and pick off as much wax as possible. Place the cloth between sheets of newspaper, brown or lining paper and iron. To remove final remnants of wax, have the batik dry-cleaned.

7 Trim the batik to size. Press, pin and zigzag stitch a double 1cm/½in turn-over down each long side and 2cm/¾in at the top and bottom. Nail the seat to the deckchair frame using upholstery pins. Start in the centre, then space the rest 2.5cm/1in apart.

Use this lovely screen as a room divider, or place it in front of a window or lamp where the light will shine through the delicate silk fabric. Various brushes and techniques give added interest.

Lightweight Folding Screen

you will need

tape measure
folding wooden screen
scissors
lightweight silk, pre-washed
silk pins (push pins)
silk-painting frame
heat-fixed (set) dyes, in lilac,
lime green and pale blue
sponge brush
hairdryer
general-purpose wax
wax pot or double boiler
tjanting
medium artist's paintbrush
coarse decorator's paintbrush
salt
iron
newspaper, brown or lining paper
narrow double-sided tape
staple gun
masking tape
strong fabric glue
ribbon or braid

1 Measure the inside edge of each panel of the screen and add at least 3cm/1¼in wastage all round. Cut the silk to size. Pin the first panel to the painting frame. Divide the length roughly in half between lilac and lime green, then apply these dyes quickly using a sponge brush and allowing the paints to blend together in the middle. Dry the silk with a hairdryer to fix (set) the dyes.

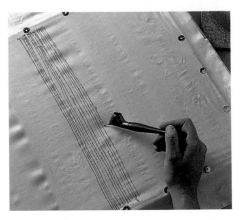

2 Heat the wax in a wax pot or double boiler (see Techniques). In the top quarter of the silk, draw fine lines of wax freehand with a tjanting. Drawing the lines freehand will add spontaneity to the design.

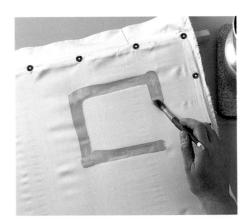

3 In the bottom quarter of the silk, draw a square of wax using a medium artist's paintbrush. You can experiment with other brushes and tools to create a variety of marks.

4 Using a coarse decorator's paintbrush, overpaint the entire panel in pale blue. Leave to dry. Paint a stripe of wax down one side of the panel.

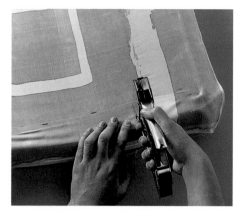

6 Remove the silk panel from the frame. Remove the wax by ironing the silk between sheets of newspaper, brown or lining paper. Prepare the remaining panels for each frame of the screen. On the first panel, run a strip of narrow double-sided tape around the inside edge of the frame (on the face of the screen).

5 Overpaint the panel again and leave to dry. Add more stripes or squares as desired. Sprinkle salt on the damp dye in some places to create an interesting textured effect. Leave to dry completely before brushing off the salt grains.

7 Stretch one of the panels across the frame, sticking it to the double-sided tape. Pull the silk tight, making sure there are no wrinkles and that the cloth is springy to the touch. The silk can be pulled up from the tape and re-stuck if adjustments are needed.

Staple the edges of the cloth evenly to the frame. Trim away any cloth that is unstuck using a pair of sharp scissors. Cover the raw edges with masking tape to prevent fraying. Using strong fabric glue, cover the untidy topside edges with ribbon or braid. Repeat to cover all the remaining frames that make up the screen.

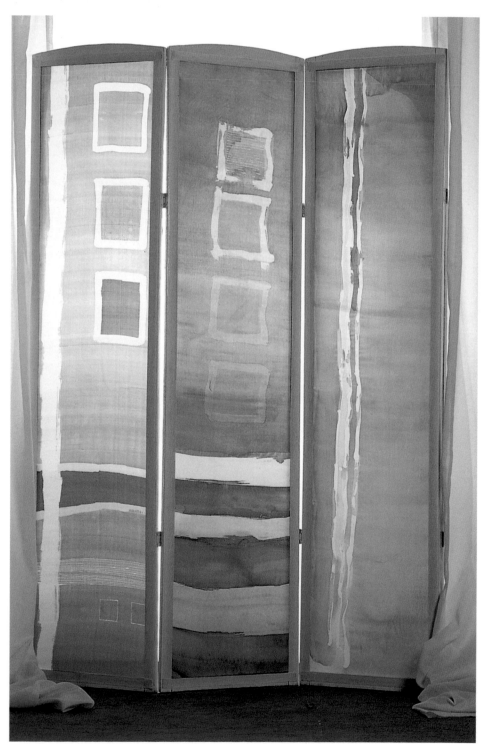

This simple design of squares within squares is drawn freehand on a measured grid to give a spontaneous look. The two-tone background fabric adds extra interest.

Vibrant Silk Cushion Cover

you will need

pencil, ruler and set square (t-square)
two-tone dupion silk, pre-washed
vanishing fabric marker
silk pins (push pins)
silk-painting frame
general-purpose wax
wax pot or double boiler
tjanting
iron-fix (set) silk paints
paintbrushes
iron
newspaper, brown or lining paper
scissors
dressmaker's pins
sewing machine
matching sewing thread
40cm/16in-square cushion pad

1 Mark a 42cm/17in square on the silk with a pencil. Mark out a grid in the centre using a vanishing fabric marker. The grid should be three squares across and three squares down, each square measuring 10cm/4in.

2 Pin the silk taut to a painting frame. It should be springy to the touch. Heat the wax in a wax pot or double boiler (see Techniques). Wax in the grid using a tjanting. It is important that there are no breaks in the outline so check the back for areas of fabric that remain opaque once the wax has been applied. Fill in any breaks with wax on the back.

3 Fill in the grid with diluted silk paints. Allow the paints to blend out from the brush to the wax outline rather than overloading the fabric with dye, as this may cause the colour to bleed underneath the wax.

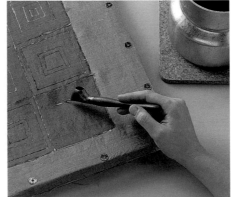

4 Leave to dry, then draw in the remainder of the design, squares within squares. Do not use a ruler for this – it will add to the effect if the squares are slightly irregular. Wax over the design lines.

5 Check the back for breaks in the outline and fill them with wax. Fill in the remaining colours using deep reds, purples, olive and brown. Use a different brush for each colour.

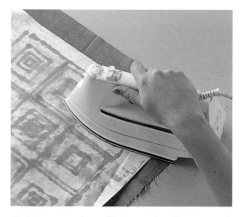

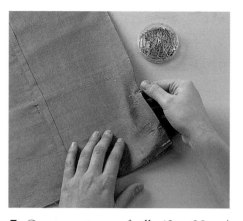

6 Remove the silk from the frame and iron out the wax between sheets of newspaper, brown or lining paper. To remove any remaining grease marks, have the finished cover dry-cleaned. Trim the fabric down to the marked 42cm/17in square.

7 Cut two pieces of silk 42 x 28cm/ 17 x 11in for the back. Stitch a double 1cm/½in hem along one long edge of each. Place the batik square right side up. Pin the two rectangles on top, face down, with the hemmed edges in the centre.

8 Stitch all the way round the cover, leaving a 1cm/½in seam allowance. Stitch a line of zigzag stitches between the sewn seam and the raw edge to prevent fraying. Turn the cover right side out and insert the cushion pad.

Decorate either end of a plain Habotai silk scarf with stripes of colour. Seal off the end of each stripe with the wax so that the colours cannot bleed into each other.

Bordered Scarf

you will need

tracing paper, soft pencil, felt-tipped pen, ruler or set square (t-square)

silk pins (push pins)

lightweight habotai silk, pre-washed

silk-painting frame

general-purpose wax

wax pot or double boiler

tjanting

iron-fix (set) silk paints

paint palette

fine artist's paintbrush

hairdryer

iron

newspaper, brown or lining paper

scissors and needle

matching sewing thread

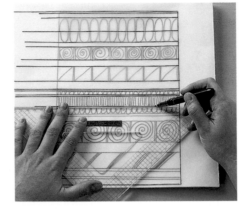

1 Enlarge the design provided at the back of the book. Trace off the horizontal lines. Pin one end of the silk to the frame. Choose a frame that is slightly deeper than the height of the border design, remembering to allow for wastage all round.

2 Turn the frame upside down on to the design and trace off all the horizontal lines, using a soft pencil. Heat the wax (see Techniques). Wax the horizontal stripes using a tjanting. Close in the ends of each stripe to prevent the paints from bleeding. The waxed lines should be semi-transparent. Wax any that aren't on the back.

3 Fill in the stripes with pale colours, such as smoky blue, terracotta or pale pink. Leave to dry. Fix (set) the silk paints using a hairdryer; be careful not to melt the wax.

4 Replace the frame upside down on the design and trace off the detail and patterning. Wax in these details with the tjanting.

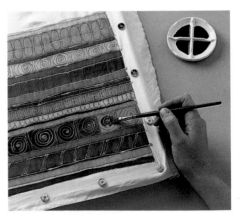

5 Paint over the stripes and details with darker colours, such as purple, blue, deep red and brown. Remove some of the hardened wax with your fingers. Repeat the process for the opposite end of the scarf.

6 Iron the batik between sheets of paper to remove the wax. The fabric will still be stiff at this stage. Trim off the wastage. If possible, tear the silk to ensure a straight edge. Roll the edges of the scarf and hand stitch. Dry-clean the finished scarf to restore the drape and sheen of the silk.

Decorate a ready made cotton napkin (or set of matching napkins) with this stylish design. Use colourfast dyes that will withstand repeated machine washing.

Geometric Napkin

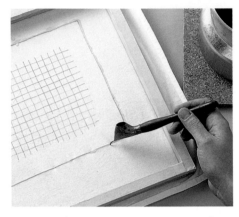

1 Draw a 10cm/4in cross in the centre of the napkin. Pin the napkin to the frame so that it is stretched taut. Draw a grid on tracing paper to fit the 10cm/4in cross. Turn the frame upside down over the design, lining up the central crosses. Trace the design on to the fabric, using a marker that will show through the fabric.

2 Heat the wax in a wax pot or double boiler (see Techniques). Draw in the main square with wax, using a tjanting. There should be no breaks in the wax outline and the cloth should appear semi-transparent. Check the back for areas of the cloth that remain opaque, and reapply the molten wax to the back.

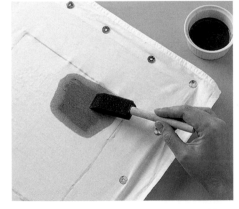

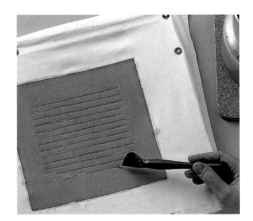

3 Using an artist's spongebrush, fill in the central square with pale blue dye. Do not overload the cloth or the colour may bleed into the white border. Allow the dye to bleed out from the brush, especially when working near the wax outline. Leave to dry.

4 When the napkin is completely dry, wax in all the horizontal lines using the tjanting. Paint the central square with lilac dye. Once again, do not overload the fabric with dye.

5 Leave to dry, then wax in all the vertical lines. Fill in the central square with cobalt blue. Remove the napkin from the frame. Place the napkin between sheets of newspaper, brown or lining paper and iron to remove the wax. Dry-clean the fabric.

This rich autumnal table runner is coloured with both paints and dyes in rich dark tones. Position the leaves at different angles to give the design a natural look.

Maple Leaf Table Runner

you will need

scissors and tape measure

dupion silk, pre-washed

tracing paper and pencil

Mylar film

craft knife and cutting mat

silk pins (push pins)

silk-painting frame

vanishing fabric marker

crackle or general-purpose wax

wax pot or double boiler

tjanting

brush (for wax)

fine artist's paintbrushes

direct-application dyes, in rusty brown and olive green

brown dye

dye bath

iron

newspaper, brown or lining paper

needle

matching sewing thread

scissors

1 Cut a piece of dupion silk to the required size, adding a 2cm/¾in seam allowance all round and 2–4cm/¾–1½in wastage. Trace the maple leaf from the back of the book, and cut out of Mylar film using a craft knife.

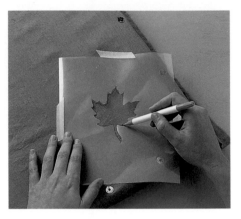

2 Pin the silk to the painting frame. Using the template and a vanishing fabric marker, draw maple leaves randomly over the cloth. Place the leaves at different angles so that they look scattered rather than neatly placed.

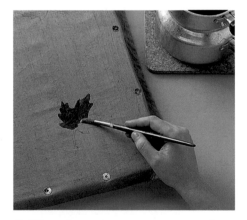

3 Heat the wax in a wax pot or double boiler (see Techniques). Using a tjanting, apply wax around the outline of some of the leaves. Block in the remaining leaves with a brush. Check the back of the fabric for breaks in the wax outline, and fill in any gaps by waxing on the back.

4 Using a small artist's paintbrush, paint in the leaves that have a wax outline with dyes. Use rusty brown and olive green colours. Leave to dry.

7 Iron the fabric between two sheets of paper until wax is no longer being absorbed. Have the fabric dry-cleaned to remove any wax residue.

5 Block in the painted leaves with wax. All the leaves should now be solidly waxed. Remove the fabric from the frame and crumple it in your hands to crack the surface of the wax.

6 Wet the batik and place it in a dark brown dye bath following the manufacturer's instructions. When the cloth is the desired colour, rinse it thoroughly. Leave to dry.

8 Using a needle, remove individual threads from opposite ends of the runner to make a fringe. Press a 1cm/½in double hem on the two remaining sides. Hem stitch each hem in place by hand. Divide the fringe at the top and bottom into equal sections and knot threads together. Trim the ends of the tassels evenly.

Decorate a plain silk tie with a simple design of stripes and dots. Use a piece of waxed string to mark out the stripes and a traditional tjanting to apply the dots.

Striped Silk Tie

you will need
general-purpose wax
wax pot or double boiler
white silk tie, pre-washed
plastic board
string
medium-spout tjanting
iron-fix (set) silk paints, in pale blue
and dark blue
medium decorator's paintbrush or
sponge brush
kitchen paper
brush (for wax)
iron
newspaper, brown or lining paper

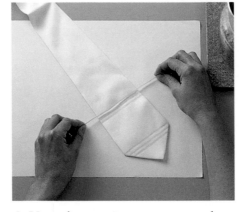

1 Heat the wax in a wax pot or double boiler (see Techniques). Place the tie on a plastic board. Put a piece of string in the wax, and leave until the wax has melted on the string. Pull the string taut, then apply the wax across the tie to create a striped pattern.

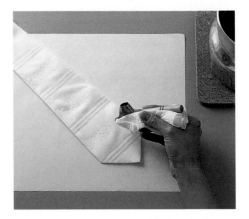

2 Using a tjanting, add dots of wax between the stripes.

3 Cover the tie with pale blue silk paint. Turn over the tie and paint on the back. Blot with kitchen paper to absorb any excess dye. Leave to dry.

4 Apply more wax with a brush across the white spots.

5 Repeat step 3 with dark blue paint. Iron the tie between sheets of paper. Continue ironing between clean sheets of paper until no more wax appears. The heat will also fix (set) the paint. Have the tie dry-cleaned to remove the excess wax.

A cheerful cup design decorates this simple cotton table mat. It is padded with a layer of wadding (batting), then hand quilted to absorb heat and protect your tabletop.

Quilted Table Mat

you will need

silk pins (push pins)

lightweight white cotton, pre-washed

painting frame

tracing paper

vanishing fabric marker

general-purpose wax

wax pot or double boiler

tjanting

medium artist's paintbrush

colourfast dyes, in sky blue, yellow, etc

iron

newspaper, brown or lining paper

scissors

medium-thickness wadding (batting)

needle

tacking (basting) thread

bias binding

dressmaker's pins

sewing machine

matching sewing thread

embroidery thread (floss)

embroidery needle

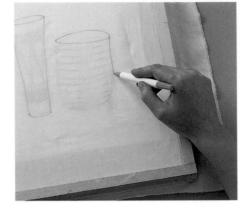

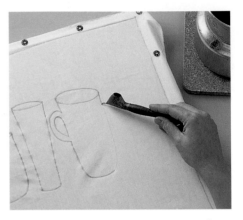

1 Pin the cotton on to the painting frame. Enlarge the template from the back of the book. Turn the frame upside down over the design and trace with a vanishing fabric marker. If the design is not visible, trace the design on to the surface of the cloth using tracing paper.

2 Heat the wax in a wax pot or double boiler (see Techniques). Using a tjanting, wax the outlines of the cups. You could also wax a line around the edge of the cloth to keep your work neat. Check the back of the fabric to make sure that the wax has penetrated through.

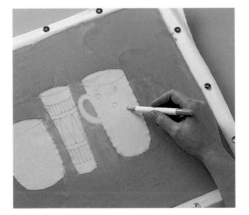

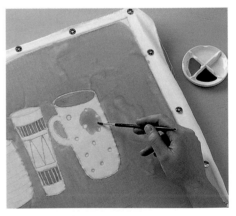

3 Using a medium artist's paintbrush, fill in the background to the cups with sky blue dye. Fill in the cup shapes with yellow dye. Do not overload the cloth with dye, as it might bleed under the wax barrier. Allow the dyes to bleed out from the brush.

4 Draw the pattern on the cups using a vanishing fabric marker. Wax in the details using the tjanting. Check the back of the fabric for breaks in the wax outline and, if necessary, reapply molten wax to the back.

5 Paint in more details, considering how one colour will affect another. Remove the batik from the frame and iron out as much wax as possible between sheets of paper. Any wax residue can be removed from cotton by boiling (see Techniques).

6 Trim the batik to the finished size. Cut a piece of wadding (batting) and a piece of backing the same size. Tack (baste) the three pieces together. Cut a length of bias binding and open out. Align the raw edge of the backing with one edge of the binding. Pin in place. Stitch down the edge of the mat, in the crease.

7 Repeat on the opposite side. Fold the binding to the right side of the mat and top stitch, close to the edge of the binding. Trim the top and bottom of the binding square with the top and bottom of the mat. Repeat on the remaining two sides of the mat, folding the ends in before stitching to give neat corners.

8 Using two or three strands of cotton embroidery thread (floss), work running stitch around the cups, stitching through all the thicknesses of the mat to produce a quilted effect.

A wax grid forms the base of this simple design, painted in muted lilac and blue colours. Crêpe de chine is used here but any lightweight silk would be equally suitable.

Square Silk Scarf

you will need

tracing paper and pencil

silk pins (push pins)

90cm/36in-square of crêpe de chine silk, pre-washed

silk-painting frame

general-purpose wax

wax pot or double boiler

medium-spout tjanting

sponge brush

iron-fix (set) silk paints, in light blue, royal blue, lilac, purple and dark blue

small bowls

brush (for wax)

kitchen paper

iron

newspaper, brown or lining paper

needle

matching sewing thread

1 Trace and enlarge the template provided. Pin the silk scarf to the frame. Turn frame side up. Place the design right side up under the corner of the silk, 7cm/3in from each side. Using a pencil, trace the design on to the back of the silk. To make the whole design, reverse the template so that the wider corner is at the outer edge. Repeat so that the wide border is around the edge of the scarf.

2 Heat the wax in a wax pot or double boiler (see Techniques). Apply the wax in spirals on the fabric using a tjanting. Keep your movements light. Make sure that the exterior of the tjanting is free of molten wax as this may smudge on to the scarf.

3 Using a sponge brush, apply light blue silk paint over the whole scarf. Allow the paint to bleed from the brush rather than overloading the fabric. Leave to dry.

4 Using a brush, apply the wax in a grid design.

5 Paint the royal blue, lilac and purple paint in the squares. Leave to dry.

6 Cover the coloured areas of the design with wax brushstrokes.

◀ **7** Apply dark blue paint over the whole scarf. Blot any excess paint with kitchen paper. Leave to dry. Iron the scarf between sheets of newspaper, brown or lining paper. The heat will also fix (set) the silk paints. Keep changing the paper until no more wax appears. Have the scarf dry-cleaned to remove the excess wax. Roll the edges of the scarf and hand stitch.

Dyeing and Marbling

Dyeing is one of the simplest ways to infuse colour into fabric, and it need not be messy. Compared to stamping, printing and fabric painting, it is much less controlled, but this unpredictability is a major part of its appeal. Each of these popular dyeing techniques gives quite different effects, offering a wide range of creative possibilities.

Colour Control

The wide range of dyes available for both hot and cold dyeing makes this method of colouring fabric as simple as it is stimulating.

In dip-dyeing, the art is often to blend colours so that they bleed together, creating a lovely feathery effect. You can also fold a napkin or handkerchief, then dip it into the dye so that just the tips of the folded edges take up the colour. Dip-dyeing is also very practical for dyeing awkward objects such as a lampshade or fake fur fabric, which could not be immersed in a dye bath.

Tie-dyeing works by preventing the dye from penetrating certain areas of the fabric. Horizontal stripes are achieved by folding or pleating the fabric; the pleats are then bound tightly with string or cord. Circular designs are made by tying round objects such as buttons, coins or lentils into the fabric, using string, cord or rubber bands. Experiment with different binding materials, as these contribute to the finished design. When the bindings and tied objects are removed after dyeing, these areas show up as plain

undyed fabric. Tie-dyeing works well on rich fabrics such as velvet and silk, or you can create striking modern effects using cotton fabrics dyed in a single bold colour. The size of each piece of tie-dyed fabric is limited to the size of the dye bath, but to make larger projects you can stitch pieces together using the patchwork technique.

Marbled fabric uses the same technique as marbled paper. Circles of marbling dye are dropped on to the surface of a shallow dye bath, then gently

dragged into decorative patterns. Again, the size of each piece of marbled fabric is limited to the size of the dye bath, so this lovely traditional fabric is

often used, like marbled paper, to cover desk sets and book covers.

Various resist mediums can be applied to fabric before dyeing. These are available in applicators with a nozzle, which makes drawing or tracing a detailed design simple. Finally, one of the most readily available of all dyes is tea, which can be brewed to any strength to give warm pale brown tones.

The most important materials used in this chapter are the dyes. Household dyes, suitable for most fabrics, are widely available. Special dye kits, including a thickening medium, are available for marbling.

Materials

dry. Remember to take the colour of the original fabric into account if you are dyeing a coloured fabric. Pre-wash fabrics to remove any dressing.

Marbling thickening medium
This solution is added to the water in the dye bath before adding marbling dyes. Carefully follow the manufacturer's instructions.

Paper
Use stiff white paper to make patchwork templates, remembering that you need to hand stitch through the paper as well as the fabric. You can also clean the marbling dyes from the dye bath with newspaper layers.

Resist medium
Painted on to areas of fabric to prevent them taking up the dye.

Absorbent cloth or paper
Use for resting dyed fabrics on to dry.

Dyes
Available in powder or liquid form. Hot-water dyes provide better colour penetration into the fibres, but may shrink the fabric, so cold-water dyes are preferable for some fabrics, such as wool and silk. Always follow the dye manufacturer's instructions. Special water-based dyes are available for marbling effects.

Fabric etching medium
Use to remove the pile from fabrics such as velvet. Available in a bottle with a nozzle for drawing designs.

Fabrics
Tie-dyeing works well on luxury fabrics such as velvet and silk, as well as on cotton fabrics. Lightweight fabrics without texture, such as fine silk or cotton, are most suitable for marbling. Unwieldy fabrics such as fake fur can be dip-dyed, then hang outdoors to

Rubber bands
Use to bind circular tie-dyed objects, to form a barrier to the dye.

Salt
Often added to a dye bath to fix (set) the dyes. Follow the dye manufacturer's instructions.

String and cord
Use to tightly bind tie-dyed objects. Experiment with various thicknesses to create different effects.

The essential piece of equipment is a dye bath. Use a bath large enough and deep enough to immerse the fabric completely so that it is evenly dyed. Work outdoors if possible.

Equipment

Cocktail stick (toothpick)

Use to pull or drag circles of marbling dye into patterns. A wooden cocktail stick (toothpick) is most suitable.

Comb

Use to create feathery marbling patterns. Make a marbling comb by taping pins to a piece of dowel.

Dye baths

Use plastic bowls or a cat litter tray for cold-water dyeing, and a heatproof metal bowl or an old saucepan for hot-water dyeing. The bath must be large enough for the fabric to be immersed completely and as flat as possible. A large, shallow dye bath is used for marbling.

Iron

Use to press pleats into fabric before tie-dyeing. Also use an iron to press the finished dyed fabric and to fix (set) the dyes, following the dye manufacturer's instructions.

Masking tape

Use to attach fabric or a design temporarily to the work surface.

Measuring jug (cup)

Use to mix dyes and marbling thickening medium before adding them to a dye bath.

Measuring spoon

Used to measure powder dyes.

Needle

Use an ordinary sewing needle for hand stitching, and an embroidery needle for embroidery thread (floss).

Paintbrush

Use a fine artist's paintbrush to drop marbling dyes on to the surface of the dye bath solution.

Pipette (eye dropper)

Use to drop marbling dyes on to the surface of the dye bath solution.

Rubber gloves

Wear rubber gloves to avoid staining your hands.

Set square (t-square)

Useful for checking accurate squares.

Vanishing fabric marker

Use to draw temporary designs on to fabric, or use tailor's chalk.

The dyeing techniques used in this chapter are all very simple to do. If you are dyeing a coloured fabric, consider how the colours will blend to create the final result.

Techniques

Making up a dye solution

Household dyes are sold in tablet form. These dyes penetrate the fibres of natural fabrics such as cotton, silk, wool and linen easily.

1 Dissolve the tablet or powder dye in the specified amount of water. Stir, then add to the dye bath.

2 Add the fabric. The dye bath should be large enough for the fabric to move freely.

3 Tea dyeing dyes fabric so that it has an antique cream colour. Place a tea bag in water until the required shade has been achieved.

Dip-dyeing

This technique is very useful if you want to dye an object such as a fabric lampshade that cannot be immersed in a dye bath. You can also use it to dye areas of fabric with more than one colour.

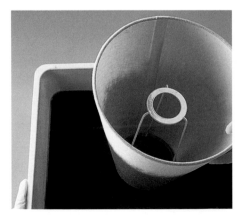

1 If you want to keep the dye colours separate, leave the fabric to dry after dipping it in the first colour and leave a small space between each colour so that the dyes cannot run together.

2 Alternatively, an attractive feathery effect can be created by dipping dip-dyed fabric into another colour while it is still slightly damp so that the two colours bleed into each other.

3 For a very simple but dramatic effect, dip just the edges of tassels or folded fabric briefly into the dye.

Tie-dyeing   The charm of this technique is its unpredictability. A great variety of designs can be achieved by folding, pleating or tying objects into the fabric so that these areas resist the colour when it is immersed in a dye bath. Experiment with scraps of fabric before embarking on a project.

To make a circular design, tie round objects such as coins, buttons or lentils into the fabric before dyeing. Bind them tightly with cord, string or rubber bands so that none of the dye can leak underneath.

To create horizontal lines, fold or pleat the fabric evenly or unevenly accordion-fashion, then bind it tightly at regular intervals.

For a lacy, speckled effect, roll the fabric round a piece of string. Pull the ends of the string round to form a loop, then slide the fabric away from the ends to make a tightly gathered circle. Tie the string ends securely.

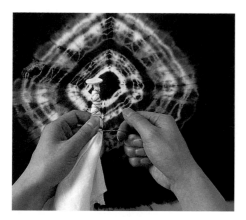

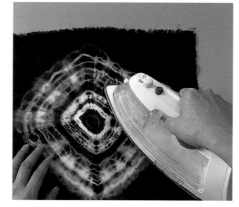

For a spider's web effect, bind a flat circular object in the fabric, then wrap string tightly around the fabric bundle. Wearing rubber gloves, prepare the dye bath using a hand dye and following the manufacturer's instructions. Use a container big enough for the fabric to be kept moving in order to achieve an even colour. Immerse the prepared fabric and move it around to ensure the dye can penetrate all areas.

When the desired colour has been achieved (it will become more intense the longer the fabric is in the dye), remove the fabric and rinse in cold water until the water runs clear. Remove the bindings, then wash the fabric in warm water with a mild detergent. Iron flat while still damp, following the dye manufacturer's instructions, to fix (set) the dye.

Marbling

Marbling fabric is similar to marbling on paper. Lightweight and untextured fabrics such as fine silk or lightweight cotton are most suitable as they quickly and evenly absorb the dye. Special marbling dyes and dye kits are available.

1 Use a dye bath deep enough for the dye solution to be at least 4–5cm/ 1½–2in deep, and large enough to arrange the fabric flat. Using a measuring jug (cup), mix the marbling thickening medium then pour it into the dye bath.

2 Using a fine artist's paintbrush or pipette (eye dropper), drop the marbling dyes on to the surface of the water. The colours will spread and float on the surface. If too much dye is used, it will sink to the bottom of the dye bath and "muddy" the solution.

3 When the surface of the dye bath is covered with colour, gently tease the surface with a fine tool such as a wooden cocktail stick (toothpick) or skewer. For a feathery texture, drag a comb lightly over the surface. Make patterns by dropping dyes of different colours on top of each other, creating large ringed circles.

4 When a pleasing pattern has been arrived at, carefully place the fabric on to the inked surface. Place either the top edge or the centre of the fabric on the surface first to prevent air bubbles from forming. When the fabric has soaked up the dye, peel it away and rinse under cool water. Leave to dry before ironing.

5 Fix (set) the dyes, following the manufacturer's instructions. This usually involves ironing the fabric on the reverse side.

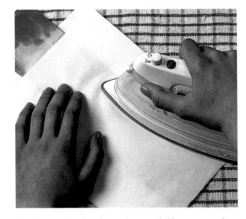

In this lovely design, the mermaids' bodies are painted with a resist medium to stop them taking up the dye, and then outlined in gold. Use cold hand dyes to give a random "watery" effect.

Mermaid Shower Curtain

you will need

scissors

8m/8yd muslin (cheesecloth)

fabric marker pen

medium artist's paintbrush

resist medium

cloth or towel

iron

sea-green cold-water dye and dye bath

gold contour-lining fabric paint

dressmaker's pins

shower curtain liner

sewing machine

matching thread

2m/2yd net curtain heading tape

2m/2yd Velcro tape

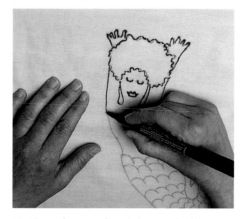

1 Cut the muslin (cheesecloth) into four pieces each 2m/2yd long and mark the position of the mermaids. Enlarge the mermaid template at the back of the book. Place each piece of muslin over the photocopy and use the fabric marker pen to draw the outline of the mermaids on to the fabric.

2 Paint the whole area of the upper body of each mermaid with resist medium. Leave to dry. Press under a cloth or towel with a hot iron for 2 minutes, to fix (set) the medium. Fold the fabric and hand dye it sea green, following the manufacturer's instructions. Iron the fabric when dry.

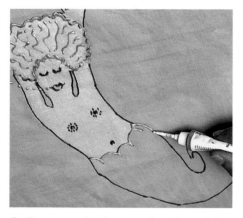

3 Paint in the hair and scales of the mermaid in gold contour paint, and add bubbles. Leave to dry flat. Pin the muslin panels together and make up to the same size as the shower curtain liner. Gather the fabric tightly on to net curtain heading tape. Attach the curtain to the liner with Velcro tape.

Dye a plain fabric lampshade in two rich colours, cherry red and terra-cotta, to create a lovely feathered effect. The beaded trim around the bottom is a perfect finishing touch.

Dip-dyed Lampshade

you will need
deep dye bath
cold water dyes, in cherry red and terracotta
rubber gloves
white linen lampshade
absorbent cloths
paper and pencil
protractor
ruler
cherry red stranded embroidery thread (floss)
large-eyed embroidery needle
12 large red glass beads
12 small beads (optional)
scissors

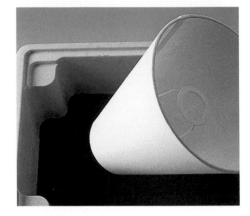

1 Using a deep dye bath, mix up the cherry red dye. Wearing rubber gloves, hold the lampshade by the base and dip it in the dye so that two-thirds of it is submerged. After a few seconds remove the lampshade. Repeat the process to intensify the colour. Stand the lampshade on an absorbent cloth.

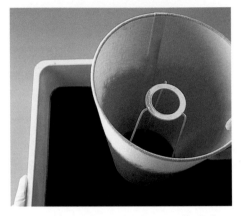

2 While the lampshade is still slightly damp, dip the top 5cm/2in in a dye bath containing terracotta dye. Stand the lampshade on an absorbent cloth to dry, allowing the second colour to bleed through the first.

3 Stand the dry lampshade upright on a piece of paper and draw around its base with a pencil. Using a protractor and ruler, divide the circle into 30° sections.

4 Stand the lampshade back on the circle, and very lightly mark the 30° sections on the bottom of the shade with the pencil.

5 Double a piece of embroidery thread (floss) and thread the loop through a needle. Push this through one of the marks on the lampshade. Take the needle through the loop and pull tight. Thread on a large bead and tie a knot 3cm/1¼in from the base of the shade. If the knot is too small and the bead slips, thread on a small bead before knotting.

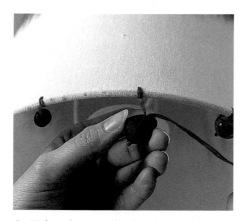

6 Take the needle back up through the large bead to hide any untidy ends, then neatly cut the thread. Following the pencil marks, repeat steps 5 and 6 until you have decorated the bottom edge of the lampshade.

Fold a small piece of silk neatly in accordion fashion and secure with rubber bands before dyeing it in a single colour. The dyed silk is then machine quilted to protect your jewellery.

Tie-dyed Jewellery Roll

you will need

dye bath

powder dye

40 x 100cm/16 x 40in wild silk

rubber bands

iron

scissors

large piece of wadding (batting)

needle

tacking (basting) thread

sewing machine

matching sewing thread

satin bias binding, in contrast colour

dressmaker's pins

15cm/6in zipper

poppers (snap fasteners)

1 Prepare a hot or cold-water dye bath of the desired colour, following the dye manufacturer's instructions.

2 Pleat the silk accordion fashion and bind it twice, using rubber bands. Dampen the bundle then place it in the dye bath. Keep the fabric moving in the dye to get an even colour.

3 When the desired colour has been achieved, remove the fabric and rinse under cold water. While the silk is still damp, remove the rubber bands and wash the fabric in warm water using a mild detergent. Iron the silk flat while it is still damp.

4 Cut two pieces 18 x 40cm/7 x 16in from the dyed silk. Cut a piece of wadding (batting) the same size and sandwich it between the two pieces of silk. Tack (baste) the layers together. Machine quilt the layers together to create a meandering quilted effect. Cut three strips of bias binding 17cm/6½in long. Position one strip along each short end of the quilted silk, fold over and pin.

5 Stitch the zipper to the underside of one short bound edge. Fold in each short end of the quilted silk by 7.5cm/3in and pin in place. Divide the end of the roll without the zipper into three equally sized pockets by stitching two lines the depth of the turn-over.

6 Position the remaining bias binding strip over the raw edge of the zipper and stitch the long sides in place.

7 For the tie, cut two strips of binding, one 20cm/8in and the other 6cm/2½in. Fold in half widthways and top stitch all around.

8 Stitch half of a popper (snap fastener) to one end of each tie. Stitch a short end of each tie to the side edges of the roll. Cut strips of bias binding to fit the long edges and pin in place Tuck in the raw edges at each end. Stitch in place, then slipstitch the short ends.

If you have a store of warm, wool blankets you no longer use on the bed, colour one softly using dye to create a beautiful throw with a luxurious velvet ribbon trim.

Velvet-edged Throw

you will need

thick wool fabric

scissors

rubber gloves

hand dye

large dye bath

iron and pressing cloth

satin bias binding

sewing machine

matching sewing thread

pins

needle

ruffled ribbon

wide velvet ribbon

1 Trim the fabric to a square or rectangular shape and wash to remove any dressing. Make up the dye in a large dye bath and check the colour on a sample piece (which you can take with you when choosing ribbons for the edging). After dyeing, rinse the fabric very thoroughly and press under a damp cloth when dry.

2 To bind the edges, machine stitch satin bias binding to the right side all round the edge. Fold the binding over to the wrong side, and baste in place. Either machine or hand stitch in place on the wrong side to finish, folding in the excess neatly at the corners.

3 On the right side, stitch a length of ruffled ribbon close to the edge of the binding to cover it. Stitch along both sides of the ribbon using matching thread.

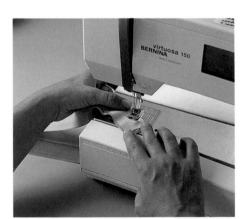

4 Cut four lengths of velvet ribbon to fit the edges of the throw. Join the lengths by stitching diagonally across each corner, with right sides together, to create mitres.

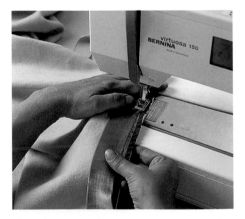

5 Pin the ribbon carefully to the throw and stitch down on each side by hand or machine. Take care when pinning velvet as it can mark easily.

Decorate the rim of a dip-dyed silk lampshade with delicate embroidery thread (floss) tassels, dip-dyeing the tip of each tassel to complement the colour used on the shade.

Tassel-edged Lampshade

you will need
dye bath
dark green cold-water dye
small silk lampshade
absorbent cloth or paper
scissors
thin cardboard
embroidery thread (floss), to match the lampshade
silk thread, to match the dye colour
small bowl
small beads
pencil or tailor's chalk
tape measure
dressmaker's glue

1 Prepare a dye bath, following the dye manufacturer's instructions. Dip the bottom edge of the lampshade briefly in the dye bath so that one-quarter is submerged. Stand it on an absorbent cloth or paper for a few minutes to remove any excess dye. Turn it upside down and leave to dry. Repeat if you would prefer to build up a darker colour.

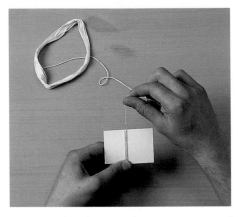

2 To make the tassels, cut a piece of thin cardboard slightly wider than the desired length of the tassels and wind the embroidery thread (floss) around it. These tassels were made by winding the thread ten times, but you can vary the number of wraps to make thicker or thinner tassels.

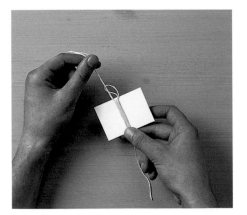

3 Cut another piece of thread about 20cm/8in long. Pass this through the loop of threads as shown. Knot the thread tightly around the loop to hold the threads tightly.

4 Using sharp scissors, cut the wrapped threads and trim evenly.

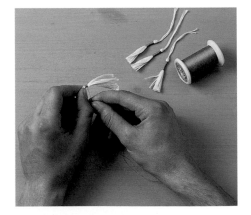

5 With a long length of coloured silk thread, bind the top of the folded-over lengths of tassel. Knot and leave the ends hanging the length of the tassel. Make enough tassels to go round the shade.

6 Prepare a dye bath slightly darker than the one used for the lampshade. Dip the tip of each tassel in the dye and leave to dry on absorbent cloth.

7 String a bead on to the looped thread at the top of each tassel, and tie a small knot to hold it in place. Cut the remaining thread down to 1cm/½in. Trim the tassels evenly.

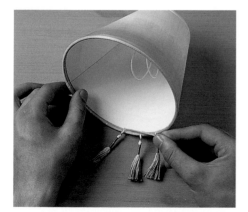

8 Using a pencil or tailor's chalk, make evenly spaced marks on the inside edge of the lampshade. Using dressmaker's glue, attach a tassel to each mark inside the rim.

Using fabric etching medium, draw a design that destroys the silk pile of velvet but leaves the backing fabric intact. The dyed velvet makes a lovely blind, with the light filtering through the etched pattern.

Velvet Blind

you will need

tracing paper and pencil
black felt-tipped pen
white silk/viscose velvet
masking tape
vanishing fabric marker
set square (t-square)
silk pins (push pins)
painting frame
fabric etching medium
hairdryer
iron
tape measure
scissors
lilac hand dye
large dye bath
rubber gloves
satin bias binding
sewing machine
matching sewing thread
roller blind kit

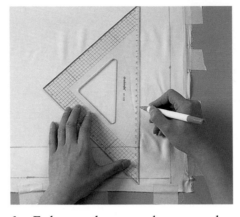

1 Enlarge the template to the required size. Outline it with a black pen . Tape the velvet, pile side down, to the work surface. Using a vanishing fabric marker and a set square (t-square), mark up the blind with a grid to fit the template.

2 Place the design underneath the velvet and trace it with the vanishing fabric marker. Move the template and repeat until the whole grid has been filled in.

3 Using silk pins, stretch the fabric on a painting frame, with the pile upwards. Trace over the design with fabric etching medium, following the manufacturer's instructions. Keep your movements fast to prevent the lines becoming too thick. (Practise on a spare piece of fabric first.)

4 Dry the etching medium with a hairdryer to burn away the pile. Once it is dry, iron the fabric on the wrong side using a cool iron. Trim any wastage from around the edge so that the velvet is the exact size required for the blind.

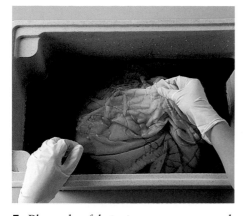

5 Place the fabric in water to reveal the design, rubbing the surface if necessary to remove unwanted fibres. Dye the blind to the required shade while the fabric is still damp, using hand dye and following the manufacturer's instructions. Hang out to dry.

6 Open up a piece of bias binding long enough to run down the side of the blind. Machine stitch it to the wrong side. Fold the binding over to the right side of the blind and top stitch close to the edge of the binding. Trim the top and bottom of the bound edge level with the top and bottom of the blind. Repeat on the other side.

7 Bind the bottom, leaving 1cm/½in extra at each end of the binding. Fold this in, then top stitch to give neat corners. Complete the blind, using a roller blind kit.

Soak pieces of blanket in tea bags and brown dye, then use them to make a soft, appealing cover for a child's hot water bottle. A drawstring cord holds the cover in place.

Tea-dyed Hot Water Bottle Cover

you will need

2–3 tea bags

dye baths

rubber gloves

old blanket or wool fabric, pre-washed

iron

cloth

brown hand dye

hot water bottle

pencil and paper

scissors

tailor's chalk

sewing machine

matching sewing thread

1.5cm/⅝in-wide brown ribbon

satin bias binding (optional)

1m/1yd fine brown cord

safety pin

vanishing fabric marker

stranded embroidery thread (floss)

embroidery needle

tiny buttons

needle

1 Soak two or three tea bags in hot water in a small dye bath until the tea is quite strong. Immerse a small piece of the old blanket or wool fabric. Agitate until you are happy with the colour, re-dyeing if necessary. Dry the fabric and press under a damp cloth.

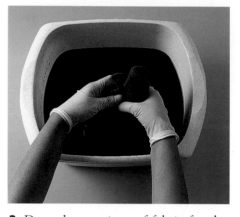

2 Dye a larger piece of fabric for the hot water bottle cover using brown hand dye and following the manufacturer's instructions. Dry and press under a damp cloth.

3 Using a hot water bottle, make a paper template for the cover. Fold the brown fabric in half and place the template on top, then draw around it with tailor's chalk. Cut out a rectangular back and front large enough to fit the hot water bottle.

4 On the wrong side of each front and back, machine stitch a length of ribbon about 5cm/2in below the top short raw edge. Using a 1cm/½in seam allowance, stitch the back and front together, leaving a gap in the stitching just below the ribbon. Fold in the top raw edge so that the ribbon is at the top edge of the bag, and stitch.

 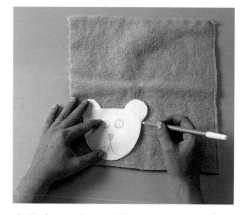 

5 Cut the cord in half. Using a safety pin, thread one piece through a side opening, around the casing and out through the same opening. Knot the ends. Repeat with the second piece of cord through the second side opening.

6 Enlarge the teddy motif at the back of the book to fit the tea-dyed fabric. Draw around the template using a vanishing fabric marker. Cut out a face. Draw in the features on the teddy's face.

7 Hand embroider the features using stranded embroidery thread (floss). Add small buttons for the eyes. Slip stitch the face to the bag front, taking care not to catch the back of the cover in the stitching.

Children will love this strong fake fur and cotton cushion, measuring 70cm/28in across x 20cm/8in high. Two contrast dye colours have been used to dip-dye the fabric.

Doughnut Floor Cushion

you will need

80cm/32in-square of paper

ruler or tape measure

50cm/20in length of string

soft pencil

scissors

dressmaker's pins

1m/1yd white acrylic fake fur fabric

1m/1yd heavy white cotton fabric

rubber gloves

cold water dyes, in turquoise and red

dye bath

sewing machine

matching sewing threads

bag polystyrene (styrofoam) pellets

large cup or beaker

1 Fold the paper into quarters. Loop the string around a pencil 7.5cm/3in from one end. Hold the end of the string in the corner of the paper and draw an arc from fold to fold. Lengthen the loop to 35cm/14in and draw another arc. Open out the pattern and pin it to the fake fur. Cut one shape. Cut another from cotton.

2 Measure the two circumferences and add 10cm/4in to each measurement. Cut three lengths of cotton, each 20cm/8in wide, two for the outside edge and one for the inside edge of the doughnut. On the wrong side of each piece of fabric, mark the halfway line with a soft pencil.

3 Wearing rubber gloves, mix each dye in a bath, following the manufacturer's instructions. Dampen each fabric piece to within 2cm/¾in of the halfway line. Dip one edge of damp fabric into the turquoise dye bath, leaving the other half outside. Remove the fabric, allowing the dye to drip back into the bath. Allow to drip dry.

4 Dip the undyed half of each piece of fabric into the red dye in the same way. Leave a 2–3cm/¾–1¼in gap between the two colours so that they do not bleed into each other.

5 With right sides together, fold one inside edge side panel in half and stitch the 20cm/8in ends together for the inner circle. Pin one edge of the inside circle to the inside edge of the fur circle. Stitch in place. Zigzag stitch the raw edges. Pin and stitch the two outer sides together into a loop. Pin and stitch the outer side to the fur circle. Turn inside out, pin and stitch the outer edge of the base to the cotton circle. Finish the edges with zigzag stitch. Carefully turn the cushion right side out.

6 Turn in the inside raw edges. Whip stitch the inside circle to the hole in the bottom of the cushion, leaving a 15cm/6in opening. Pour in the polystyrene (styrofoam) pellets to fill the cushion. Stitch the opening shut.

Dip-dyeing lengthways and then widthways creates subtle blends of colour, but choose your colours carefully to avoid a "muddy" effect. Finish these simple mats with contrast ribbon borders.

Double-dyed Place Mats

you will need

scissors

white cotton fabric

cold water hand dyes, in 3 colours

large dye bath

rubber gloves

clothes pegs (pins)

iron

ribbon, in contrast colours

dressmaker's pins

needle

tacking (basting) thread

embroidery thread (floss)

needle

1 Cut the fabric to the desired size for each mat, cutting along the grain of the fabric to ensure a square edge. The fabric may fray during dyeing, so allow 1–2cm/½–¾in wastage. Prepare the first dye bath following the manufacturer's instructions. Dampen the fabric with water.

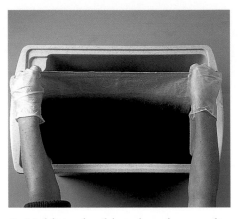

2 Holding the fabric lengthways, dip each rectangle no more than two-thirds into the bath. When the fabric is the desired colour (it will become more intense the longer it is in the dye), remove it and rinse in cold water until the water runs clear.

3 Prepare the second dye bath. While the fabric is still damp, dip each rectangle in the dye bath lengthways so that the undyed area is submerged. Prepare the third dye bath.

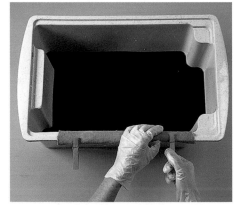

4 Dip each mat widthways so that half of it is submerged. Peg (pin) the fabric to the edge of the dye bath. This colour will cover both of the previously dyed colours, creating subtle colour blends. Wash the mats using a mild detergent, and rinse until the water runs clear. Iron while damp.

5 Trim the edges of each mat. Press the ribbon in half lengthways and pin around the outside of the mat so that the crease lies on the edge. Tack (baste) in place. Using embroidery thread (floss), work blanket stitch through the edge of the ribbon to hold it in place. Remove the tacking.

To create this tie-dye design on plain handkerchiefs, simply fold them then dip the edges of the pleated folds briefly in two dye colours. The result is a striking chequerboard pattern.

Folded Silk Handkerchiefs

you will need
white or pale-coloured silk
handkerchiefs, pre-washed
iron
dye bath
powder dyes, in 2 colours
absorbent cloth or paper
brown craft or lining paper

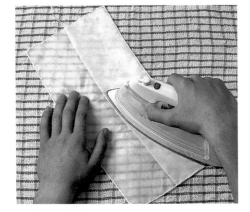

1 Wash each piece of fabric in mild detergent to remove any dressing. Pleat the handkerchief accordion-style into quarters and press the folds.

2 Prepare a dye bath with the first colour dye, following the manufacturer's instructions. You will only need a small amount of dye. Turn each pleated handkerchief so that a row of folds points down, then dip the edge very briefly in the dye.

3 Place each handkerchief on an absorbent piece of cloth or paper, then carefully open out flat to dry. Place each handkerchief flat between two pieces of brown craft or lining paper, and press with a warm, dry iron. Remove from the paper.

4 Pleat the handkerchiefs with the folds at right angles to the previous ones, across the lines of dye. Press each fold. Prepare the dye bath with the second colour, then dip the handkerchiefs as before. Leave to dry and press as in step 3.

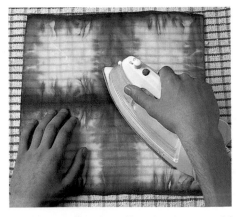

5 Rinse the handkerchiefs in cold water until the water runs clear. Then wash in lukewarm water using a mild detergent. Iron the handkerchiefs flat while still damp.

Cover a selection of notebooks, a shoebox and a cardboard tube with marbled fabric to make a co-ordinating desk set. The metal fittings add a traditional look.

Marbled Fabric Desk Set

you will need
large shallow dye bath
marbling thickening medium
rubber gloves
marbling dyes, in black and white
small pointed instrument such as
a skewer
scissors
cotton sateen fabric
double-sided tape
2 short lengths of square
wooden dowel
notebooks, shoebox and large
cardboard tube
strong fabric glue
metal label frames
bradawl
pop rivet tool and metal rivets

1 Fill the dye bath with cold water to a depth of about 5cm/2in. Add the marbling thickening medium. Wearing rubber gloves, drop a small amount of black marbling paint on to the surface.

2 Drop a small amount of white marbling paint on to the surface of the black paint.

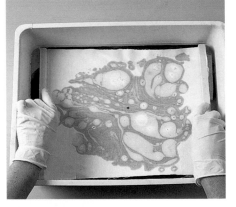

4 Cut the fabric into rectangles that will fit into the dye bath. Using double-sided tape, attach each end of the first piece of fabric to a length of wooden dowel; this will hold the fabric flat and make it easier to handle. Holding the dowels, gently arrange the fabric, right side down, on to the surface of the water.

5 Lift the fabric carefully, then untape the dowels and hang up to dry. Repeat with the remaining fabric until you have enough to cover the desk set.

3 Using a small pointed instrument, gently mix the two colours into a swirly marbled pattern.

6 To cover the large notebook, apply strips of double-sided tape to the book cover. Take a piece of fabric about 5cm/2in larger all round than the notebook and wrap it around it, pressing firmly. Snip across each corner. Apply fabric glue to the exposed edges, then stick them to the inside. Place a metal label frame on the front. Pierce a hole through each fixing (attachment) point, using a bradawl. Use a pop rivet tool and rivets to hold the metal frame in place.

7 For the pen pot, cut a piece of fabric 5cm/2in deeper than the cardboard tube and 1cm/½in longer than its circumference. Fold and glue a small hem along the lower edge. Apply fabric glue to the tube, then wrap the fabric round it. Glue down the overlap. Snip tabs into the excess fabric at the top. Apply glue to the inside of the tube, then fold the tabs into the inside.

This pretty little crêpe de chine bag could be used to hold cosmetics or jewellery. If this is one of your first marbling projects, dye several pieces of fabric and choose the best.

Marbled Drawstring Bag

you will need

scissors

0.25m/¼yd silk crêpe de chine

large shallow dye bath

marbling thickening medium

rubber gloves

marbling dyes, in red, yellow and green

needle or toothpick

iron

0.25m/¼yd fine cotton, for the lining

dressmaker's pins

sewing machine

matching sewing thread

ribbon or cord

1 Cut the crêpe de chine into pieces 25 x 15cm/10 x 6in. Fill the bath with 3–5cm/1–2in of water and add the marbling thickening medium. Wearing rubber gloves, drop a little of each dye on to the surface. The colours will spread out and run into each other to cover the surface.

2 Using a needle or toothpick, make swirls and spirals. Be careful not to overmix the colours.

3 Place a piece of fabric carefully on to the marbled surface, allowing one end to touch the surface first.

4 Peel the fabric away from the surface. Rinse gently in cold water to remove the thickening medium, then dry flat. Repeat with the other pieces of fabric. Iron on the back to fix (set) the dyes. Choose the best two pieces for the outer bag and discard the rest.

5 Cut two pieces of lining 25 x 15cm/ 10 x 6in to match the size of the marbled fabric. Place one piece of lining and one piece of marbled fabric wrong sides together and pin. Repeat. On one end of each piece of marbled fabric, fold over 5cm/2in and pin.

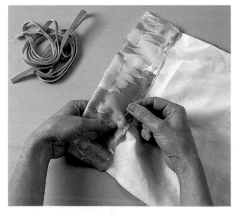

6 Pin a channel 4cm/1½in from the fold and machine stitch. With marbled sides together, machine stitch the sides and bottom of the bag, leaving the channel open. Turn right side out and thread ribbon or cord through the channel.

Quilt a piece of marbled silk fabric so that it will hold a pair of spectacles safely. Decorate the diagonal quilting pattern with small rocaille beads, and finish with ribbon roses around the top.

Marbled Spectacle Case

you will need

shallow dye bath 30cm/12in square

marbling thickening medium

fine artist's paintbrush

marbling dyes

wooden cocktail stick (toothpick)

ruler

scissors

silk, pre-washed

iron

wadding (batting)

cotton lining

needle

tacking (basting) thread

vanishing fabric marker

sewing machine

matching sewing thread

dressmaker's pins

narrow ribbon

5mm/¼in rocaille beads

6 ribbon roses

1 Prepare a shallow dye bath and add the marbling thickening medium. Scatter drops of dye on to the surface. Drag a toothpick through the dyes at intervals, first horizontally then vertically, to create a feathery pattern.

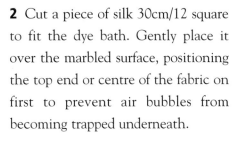

2 Cut a piece of silk 30cm/12 square to fit the dye bath. Gently place it over the marbled surface, positioning the top end or centre of the fabric on first to prevent air bubbles from becoming trapped underneath.

3 When the silk has soaked up the dye, carefully peel it away and rinse under cool water to remove the thickening medium. Leave to dry, then press with a warm, dry iron to fix (set) the dyes, following the manufacturer's instructions.

4 Cut the wadding (batting) 30cm/12in square, and the lining slightly larger. Place the lining on the work surface, centre the wadding on top, then the silk. Tack (baste) the layers together, in rows 3cm/1¼in apart. Using a vanishing fabric marker, draw a diagonal grid across the surface with the lines 2.5cm/1in apart.

5 Machine stitch along the marked lines to quilt the fabric. Cut a 20cm/8in square from the finished piece and fold in half, right sides together. Pin along the side and bottom edges, then machine stitch 1cm/½in from the edge. Neaten with zigzag stitch then turn right side out.

6 Cut a 20cm/8in length of ribbon, press in half and stitch over the raw edges. Hand sew a rocaille bead at every point where two quilting lines cross. Hand sew ribbon roses below the opening.

Use a small piece of marbled silk to cover a ready-made headband. The silk is cut on the cross grain so that it will stretch round the curved shape of the headband.

Marbled Headband

you will need
shallow dye bath
marbling thickening medium
fine artist's paintbrush
marbling dyes
wooden cocktail stick (toothpick)
silk, pre-washed
iron
scissors
padded wire headband
dressmaker's pins
clear adhesive

1 Prepare a shallow dye bath and add the marbling thickening medium, following the manufacturer's instructions. Using a fine artist's paintbrush, scatter drops of dye on to the surface. When the surface is covered with colour, drag a cocktail stick or toothpick through the dye at regular intervals, vertically then horizontally, to break up the dye and create a pattern.

2 Gently place the silk on to the marbled surface, placing the top or the centre on first. When the silk has soaked up the dye, peel it away and rinse under cool water to remove the thickening medium. Leave to dry, then iron to fix (set) the dye, following the manufacturer's instructions.

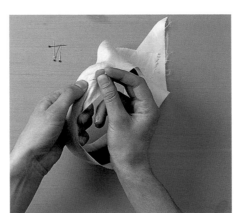

3 Cut a strip of the marbled silk diagonally across the grain, at least twice the width of the headband.

4 Remove the lining from the inside curve of the headband, and pin the strip of silk to one end. Stretching the fabric gently around the outside of the curve, pin the other end of the silk to the other end of the headband.

5 Trim the edges to 2cm/¾in wider than the headband on each side. Coat the inside curve of the headband with adhesive, then glue the raw edges down, mitring the corners. Glue the original lining back in position.

In this complex marbling design, extra colours are added on top of each other and then carefully dragged out to create petal-like shapes. The background marbling is done using a handmade comb.

Marbled Book Cover

you will need

masking tape
dressmaker's pins
wooden batten or ruler
shallow dye bath
marbling thickening medium
marbling dyes
pipette (eye-dropper)
fine artist's paintbrush
wooden cocktail stick (toothpick)
scissors
crêpe de chine silk, pre-washed
tape measure
book, photo album or diary
absorbent cloth or paper
iron
tape
sewing machine
matching sewing thread
needle

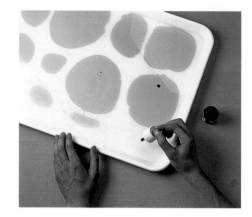

1 Make a comb for marbling a feathery pattern by taping dressmaker's pins along the edge of a wooden batten or a ruler. Prepare a shallow dye bath with marbling thickening medium (see Techniques). Using a pipette (eye-dropper), place eight drops of each background dye colour on to the surface, allowing room for each colour to spread.

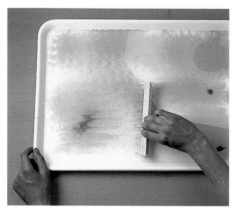

2 Carefully drag the homemade comb several times across the surface, backwards and forwards, horizontally and vertically, to create a feathery pattern.

3 Add to the design by applying drops of a contrasting colour dye to the surface of the dye bath, allowing them to spread outwards.

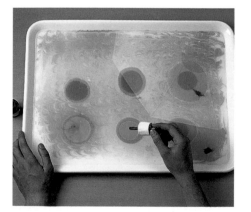

4 Apply different-coloured drops to the centre of each circle.

5 Continue applying colour to the centre of each circle, until you have as many colours as you want.

6 Around each circle, drag the point of a toothpick from the outside edge towards the centre, to form petal-like shapes. Drag the point of the stick from within the petals past the outside edges to create points.

7 Cut two pieces of fabric 1.5cm/⅝in larger than the opened book size. Place each in turn on the surface of the inked solution.

8 When the silk has soaked up the dye, peel it away and rinse under cool water to remove the thickening medium. Place on absorbent cloth or paper to dry, then press with a warm, dry iron to fix (set) the dye, following the manufacturer's instructions.

9 Place one piece of silk right side down. Centre the opened book, cover side down on top. Fold the fabric edges in and tape them to the inside of the cover, mitring the corners.

10 For the book flaps, from the remaining dyed silk, cut two pieces, each the size of the inside cover plus 2cm/1in seam allowances all around. Press under a 1cm/½in seam all round, then stitch the fold along one short edge. With right sides together and raw edges aligned, pin each flap to the outside edges of the outer cover. Ensure the machine-stitched edge faces the centre of the book. Hand stitch the other three sides in place.

Neatly pressed pleats create this simple design, which is then bound with fine cord or string to create the tie-dye effect. Only one shade of dye is used on coloured fabric.

Pleated Table Runner

you will need

iron

lilac silk dupion, pre-washed

ruler

scissors

fine cord or string

rubber gloves

dye bath

blue hand dye

needle

matching sewing thread

1 Iron the washed silk while still damp. Cut to the size required for your table (the length should include the fringe), allowing 4.5cm/1¾in wastage on all sides.

2 Using an iron, pleat the fabric accordion fashion, making each pleat about 3cm/1¼in wide. If your runner is very long, horizontal pleats may become unmanageable, so you may prefer to make the pleats vertically.

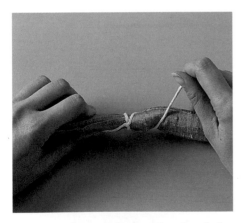

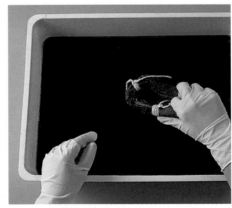

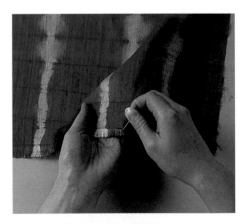

3 Using fine cord or string, bind the fabric tightly along the length of the pleats, spacing each binding about 7.5cm/3in apart. Start in the centre and work out towards the edges.

4 Wearing rubber gloves, prepare a dye bath large enough to allow the fabric to move freely. Dampen the tied cloth before placing it in the bath. Dye the fabric according to the manufacturer's instructions. When it is the desired colour, remove it and rinse under cold water until the water runs clear. Remove the bindings and wash to remove any dye.

5 Iron flat while still damp. Using a needle, make a fringe at each short end by pulling out the weft threads to about 4cm/1½in deep. Fold the cloth in half to ensure that it is square, then trim 2.5cm/1in from each long side. Press under a 1cm/½in double hem on each long side, then slip stitch it neatly in place. Trim the ends of the fringe level at each end.

Machine stitch large blue-and-white tie-dyed squares on to a plain white duvet cover for a bold modern look. Vary the stripes and circles to add extra interest to the design.

Tie-dyed Duvet Cover

you will need

iron

white cotton and linen fabrics with contrasting textures, pre-washed

coins, marbles and beads

rubber bands

strong thread or string

blue machine or hand dye

dye bath (optional)

set square (t-square)

scissors

needle

tacking (basting) thread

white duvet cover

vanishing fabric marker

dressmaker's pins

sewing machine

matching sewing thread

1 Iron the cotton and linen fabrics flat while still damp. Tie circular items of different sizes, such as coins, marbles or beads, into half of the fabric pieces, securing them tightly with rubber bands.

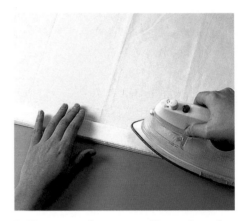

2 To create the stripe effect, pleat the remaining fabric accordion fashion, with the pleats about 3cm/1¼in wide. Bind the pleated roll of fabric, using strong thread or string. Space the ties evenly on each piece of fabric, but vary the spacing between pieces of cloth to give interesting stripes of different proportions.

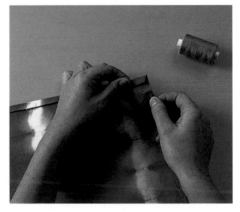

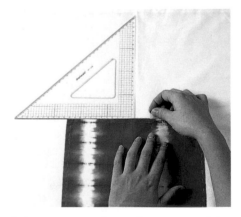

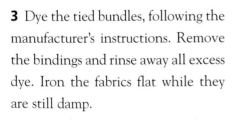

3 Dye the tied bundles, following the manufacturer's instructions. Remove the bindings and rinse away all excess dye. Iron the fabrics flat while they are still damp.

4 Cut the dyed fabrics into 27cm/ 11in squares, which includes a 1cm/½in seam allowance on all sides. Turn under the seam allowance and tack (baste), mitring the corners neatly. Press each square.

5 Iron a crease down the centre of the duvet cover. Measure and mark with a vanishing marker 25cm/10in down the central crease from the top seam. Centre the first square on the crease, with the top edge on the 25cm/10in mark. Pin in position.

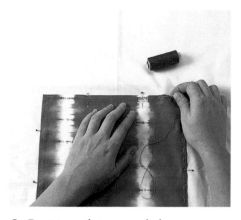 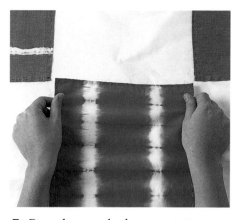 

6 Position the rest of the top row, placing them one square's width from each other horizontally. Tack (baste) in place.

7 Pin, then tack the remaining tie-dyed squares, making sure they are all square to each other and to the sides of the duvet cover.

8 Machine stitch round each square close to the edge. Remove the tacking threads. Wash the cover according to the dye manufacturer's instructions.

Tie-dyeing works well on rich fabrics such as velvet and silk-satin. Bind patches of different fabrics round circular objects such as buttons and beads, then assemble the patchwork by hand.

Tie-dyed Patchwork Cushion

you will need
small piece of cardboard
ruler
scissors
selection of light-coloured fabrics (e.g.
velvet, silk dupion, silk-satin)
vanishing marker pen
coins, lentils, buttons and beads
rubber bands
rubber gloves
cold water hand dyes, in 4 colours
dye bath
iron
stiff paper
dressmaker's pins
needle
tacking (basting) thread
matching sewing thread
cushion pad

1 Divide the dimensions of the cushion front and back by the required number of patches. Add on 2cm/¾in all round and cut out a cardboard template to that size. Cut the required number of squares using the template as a guide. In the centre of each, place a circular object such as a button or coin and bind securely with a rubber band. Divide the bundles into four, putting a mix of fabrics in each pile.

2 Wearing rubber gloves, prepare each dye bath following the dye manufacturer's instructions, then immerse the bundles for the specified length of time. Rinse in cold water until the water runs clear. Remove the bindings and wash the squares in warm water using mild detergent.

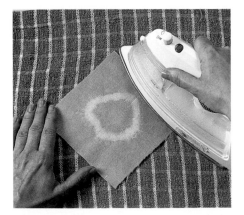

3 Iron the fabric flat while still damp. Trim the fabric squares by 1cm/½in all around.

4 Cut away 2cm/¾in all around the cardboard template. Use it to make paper templates. Centre a template on the wrong side of each square. Fold in the excess fabric and pin.

5 Mitre the corners and tack (baste) around the edge, stitching through the fabric and the paper. Arrange the squares into a rectangle four squares wide by eight squares long, which, when folded in half, will make up the front and back of the cushion cover. Ensure that you are happy with the arrangement of colours.

6 Oversew all the squares right sides together. Sew the mitred corners in place, except on those that appear around the outside edge of the rectangle. Remove the tacking threads and the templates, then press the seams flat under a damp cloth. Fold the patchwork in half, right sides together, and stitch along two sides.

7 Fold over the seam allowance on the open side and tack. Turn the cover through to the right side and insert the cushion pad. Pin, then sew the open side closed.

Make a set of fine cotton napkins using just one colour of dye and hand folding the fabric into small pleated parcels. Make a tablecloth or tablemats to match if you like.

Folded Napkin Parcels

you will need

scissors

ruler or set square (t-square)

fine white cotton fabric

dressmaker's pins

needle

tacking (basting) thread

sewing machine

white sewing thread

large bodkin or safety pin

iron

thick string

hand dye

glass bowl (for microwave method)

clear film (plastic wrap) (for microwave method)

dye bath (for hand method)

rubber gloves

1 Cut six squares each 35cm/14in and six strips 35 x 5cm/14 x 2in from the cotton fabric. Pin under a narrow double hem on all four sides of each square. Fold each strip in half lengthways and tack (baste), then machine stitch about 1cm/½in from the raw edge, leaving a small gap in the stitching halfway along the length. Use a large bodkin or safety pin to turn each strip to the right side. Press flat. Stitch the gap.

2 Find the centre of each strip and pin it to one edge of each square, about halfway along. Stitch the hem in place close to the innermost folded edge, stitching over the strip. Press the hem.

5 Prepare a dye bath following the manufacturer's instructions and microwave for four minutes. Alternatively leave the parcels submerged for 45 minutes. Wearing rubber gloves, remove the parcels and rinse. Remove the string and rinse again until the water runs clear. Iron while still damp.

3 Fold each napkin into pleats about 4cm/1½in wide, then press flat using your hands.

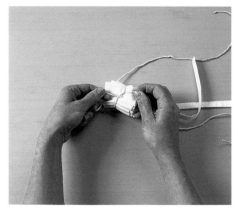

4 Fold each pleated napkin again to form a small square parcel. Tie up the napkin parcel tightly using a length of thick string.

Tie-dyed silk fabrics make a luxurious lightweight bedcover. Vary the objects tied into the patches and the binding materials, as well as the size of the patches.

Tie-dyed Patchwork Bedspread

1 To make a bedspread 1.5 x 1.8m (5 x 6ft), you will need three patch sizes: 15 squares each 30cm/12in, 30 squares each 15cm/6in, and 30 rectangles 30 x 15cm/12 x 6in. Make a paper template as a guide, then cut the required number from fabric adding a 1cm/½in seam allowance all round.

2 Tie different circular objects into the fabric patches. Bind them with various cords and strings to vary the tie-dyed results.

3 Prepare each dye bath, following the manufacturer's instructions, and dye one-quarter of the material in each bath. Wash each patch in warm water, using a mild detergent. Remove the objects and rinse until the water runs clear. Leave to dry on absorbent cloth or paper.

4 Steam iron each patch. Turn in each seam allowance using a paper template as a guide. Pin and tack (baste) the seam firmly in place.

5 Using a neat overstitch, hand stitch two small patches together to make a rectangle. Continue joining the small squares together until you have 15 bicoloured rectangles.

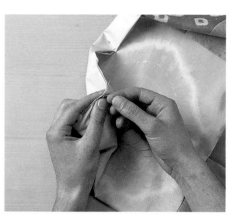

6 Sew a pieced rectangle to a single rectangle, to form a 30cm/12in square. Continue joining rectangles until you have a total of 15 squares. Sew a patchwork square to a solid square.

7 Continue joining squares in this way to make a row of five squares, alternating patchwork squares with solid ones. Arrange in six rows, starting three rows with a patched square and three with a solid one. Sew the rows together. Remove the tacking threads and the paper templates. Press the seams flat. Pin the backing fabric to the patchwork, right sides together. Machine stitch round three sides. Turn the bedspread through, then pin and stitch the open side closed.

Space-dyeing

Natural fabrics and yarns can be dyed with several colours at once, giving wonderful random rainbow colours and magical effects. Once you have experimented with ready-made dyes, you can progress to making up your own dye recipes. Dyes can be painted on to the fabric with a brush, sprayed on with a water mister or sprinkled using a pepperpot. Alternatively, dampened fabric can be coloured in a dye bath with several colours together.

Random Reactions

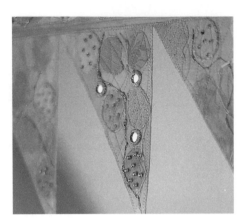

In most dyeing techniques the aim is to submerge the fabric completely with plenty of room in the dye bath so that the fibres take up the colour even-ly. Space-dyeing employs a different technique. By deliberately crumpling the fabric instead of spread-ing it out, and using several different colour dyes at once in the same dye bath, a random multi-coloured pattern will emerge. The more the fabric is crumpled, the greater the patterning will be. Until the dyeing is completed and the fabric is dry, the outcome cannot be predicted so this technique is stimulating to experiment with.

To make sure all the fabric is dyed you need to cover all the white parts with the various dye solutions, but do not stir them together in case the colours merge and become "muddy". Different kinds of

dye are suitable for different fabrics – acid dyes (where the acid is a white vinegar), for instance, are used for wool and silk, but not for cotton or linen. Fabrics such as silk react very quickly to the dye, while others take much longer. Space-dyeing

produces vibrant colours on fabrics such as cotton and silk, but used on a delicate fabric such as muslin (cheesecloth) it will give a pastel look. Follow the instructions in the Techniques section for achieving pale or deep colours, as specified in each project.

As well as space-dyeing fabrics, embroidery threads (floss) and woollen yarns can also be dyed. These random-dyed threads look wonderful mixed together in a piece of embroidery. Reactive dyes can be painted directly on to the fabric, then sealed

in a plastic bag to fix (set). Alternatively, spray on the dyes, using cut-out

paper shapes or bands of tape to mask off areas of plain fabric to make a design.

If you are using a dye bath, this will dictate the size of the fabric you can dye, so if you have only a small dye bath, create larger finished projects by using the patchwork technique to join fabric pieces together. Another idea is to decorate a large area of plain fabric such as a tablecloth or pelmet with small pieces of spray-dyed fabric.

The appeal of space-dyeing is its random colouring effect. The dye bath for this technique need not be large, as fabric is crumpled to allow the different dyes to blend together in the fabric.

Materials

Beads
Use these for decoration.

Bonding powder (fusible web)
This is used to bond two fabrics together with heat.

Dyes
Acid dyes (using white vinegar) are used for wool and silk, cold-water reactive dyes for cotton, viscose and silk. Special fabric paints and printing inks are also available.

Fabrics
These include natural and manmade fabrics such as cotton poplin, wool and silk. All cotton, except velvet, should be machine washed at 60°C/140°F, then dried. Wool and silk should be dampened in warm water with washing-up liquid added before dyeing.

Non-woven interfacing
Available in a range of weights, including pelmet weight.

Polyester toy stuffing
Light and resilient, this can be used for stuffing small shapes.

Salt
Common salt is needed for some reactive dyeing methods.

Threads (floss) and yarns
Try dyeing silk and wool thread for embroidery, or cotton lace, viscose cord and cotton or viscose fringing for sewing projects.

Urea
This is used in solution to help dissolve the dye in strong solutions. It also allows greater dye penetration when spray-dyeing and fabric painting with reactive dyes.

Washing soda (sodium carbonate)
Use washing soda to fix reactive dyes. Dissolve 100g/3½oz washing soda crystals in 500ml/18fl oz boiling water. Stir well and allow to cool.

Washing-up (dishwashing) liquid
Use to soak fabric and threads before dyeing, and for setting cotton. A neutral pH detergent is useful, as it prevents any unfixed dye being picked up by another part of the fabric.

White vinegar
This is used to fix acid dyes.

While fabric that is dyed using space-dyeing methods appears spontaneous, the dyes and chemical solutions are carefully weighed out. Accurate measuring equipment is very important in space-dyeing.

Equipment

Baking paper (parchment paper)
Protect the ironing board with a cloth while ironing fabric dry. Use baking paper to protect the iron.

Clothes pegs (pins)
Use to seal dyed fabric in plastic bags.

Dye bath
Dye baths for cold-water reactive dye methods can be plastic. Use a heat-proof container for hot-water dyes. Use a metal dye bath for acid dyes.

Glass jars with lids
Use to make and store dye solutions.

Iron
Press damp dyed fabrics dry. Use to press fabrics.

Measuring beaker
Use to measure dye solutions and add water to make up volume.

Measuring spoon
Use to measure dye powders.

Pepperpot (pepper shaker)
Use to sprinkle reactive dyes on to dampened fabric.

Plastic bags
Use to seal a dye bath, using clothes pegs (pins).

Plastic piping
Use to roll up dye-painted fabric before sealing in a plastic bag.

Plastic sheet
Use a large plastic sheet to protect your work surface, especially when painting with dyes.

Rubber gloves
Wear to avoid staining your hands.

Scales and measuring spoons
Use scales to weigh dry fabric. Use measuring spoons for dyes and beakers and syringes for measuring liquids.

Stirring rods
Use glass or plastic rods, or lengths of bamboo, to mix dye solutions.

Syringe
Use to measure very accurate quantities of dye solution.

Thermometer
Use to check temperature of hot water dye bath while heating.

When space-dyeing with cold water dyes, it is best to use no more than 3–4 times the volume of liquid to the weight of the fabric. To dye 100g/3½oz fabric, use up to 400ml/14fl oz total liquid.

Techniques

Preparing soda solution and cold-water reactive dyes

Cold water reactive dyes remain usable for about a week after they have been made up. After that they lose strength. Store in a sealed jar.

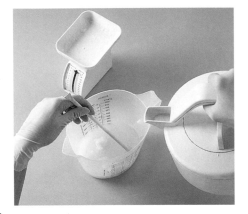

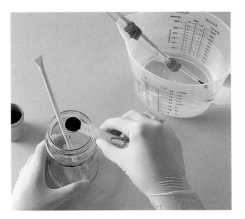

1 To make a soda solution, dissolve 100g/3½oz washing soda crystals (sodium carbonate) in 500ml/18fl oz boiling water. Stir well then leave to cool.

2 To make a stock dye solution, pour 300ml/½ pint cold water into a glass jar, mark the level around the jar and pour the water away.

3 Measure 2.5ml/½ tsp dye powder into the jar. Add a few drops of cold water and stir to a paste. Pour hot water (not more than 60°C/140°F) into the jar up to the mark and stir thoroughly until the dye is dissolved.

Pepperpot (pepper shaker) method with reactive dyes

The pepperpot method of dyeing fabric produces a subtle speckled effect of comets and tails on the fabric surface.

1 Dissolve 25g/1oz salt in 100ml/3½fl oz hot water. Leave to cool, then measure 25ml/1½ tbsp salt solution and 40ml/1½fl oz soda solution into a jar. Make the mixture up to 150ml/¼ pint with cold water.

2 Cut a piece of dry fabric from your project instructions to fit into the bottom of a deep plastic tray. Paint with the salt and soda solution until damp but not too wet.

3 Put small amounts of up to three powdered cold-water reactive dyes into pepperpots (pepper shakers).

4 Shake the dye sparingly on to the fabric, a small amount at a time. Leave for a minute between applications, as the colour will develop quite quickly. Leave for 30 minutes to 1 hour. Remove the fabric from the dye bath and rinse until the water runs clear. Wash in hot soapy water, then rinse again. Iron the fabric dry.

Cold-water reactive space-dyeing method for pale colours

When fabric has been coloured with reactive dyes, rinse it thoroughly until the water runs clear. Wash in water with washing up (dishwashing) liquid, leave to dry partially, then iron dry.

1 Weigh the fabric to be dyed, then soak in warm water with a little washing-up (dishwashing) liquid added for at least 30 minutes. Squeeze out the excess water and crumple the fabric in the dye bath.

2 For each colour used, measure the amount of dye solution needed with a syringe and pour into a measuring beaker. Refer to the recipe, and add the amount of water required

3 Measure the soda solution (sodium carbonate) needed and pour into the beaker containing dye solution. Once this has been added, the dye solution must be used fairly quickly, as it will lose its strength within a couple of hours of making.

4 Pour the solutions carefully over the fabric in the dye bath. (Dye baths for cold water reactive dye methods can be plastic.) Try to cover all white parts, but do not stir or the colours may become muddy.

5 Leave for at least one hour at room temperature, then rinse thoroughly until the water runs clear. Wash in hot water with a little washing-up liquid added, then rinse again. Allow the fabric to dry partially and then iron completely dry. It is ready for use after airing.

Spray-dyeing

Measure 2.5ml/½ tsp dye into a glass. Stir to a paste with cold water. Make up to 300ml/½ pint with chemical water and stir well. Measure 20ml/4 tsp of this solution into a spray bottle. Add an equal amount of soda solution. Spray the fabric, allowing a few minutes' rest between colours to let the colour spread. Spray evenly over the whole piece, or concentrate colours in particular areas. Areas may be masked by pinning paper shapes to the fabric after one colour has been sprayed and then spraying another colour. Remove the masks and allow the fabric to dry overnight. Press with a hot iron. Wash the fabric in hot soapy water, allow to dry then iron again.

Cold water reactive space-dyeing method for deep colours

If very strong solutions or dyes are needed, you may prefer to make them up in chemical water. This helps the dye to dissolve but does not affect the colour or depth of shade.

1 If very strong solutions of dye are needed, you may prefer to make them up in chemical water. This helps the dye dissolve but does not affect the colour or depth of shade. To make chemical water, weigh out 120g/4oz urea and make up to 1 litre/1¾ pints with hot water. Stir well and allow to cool. Make the dye into a paste with cold water, then make up to 300ml/½ pint with chemical water.

2 Spread out the fabric in a plastic dye bath. The more crumpled the fabric is, the greater the patterning will be.

3 Measure the chemical dye solution according to the recipe and add the soda solution (sodium carbonate) as before. Pour the solutions carefully over the fabric in the dye bath, trying to cover all white parts. Do not stir unless asked to do so, as three-colour mixtures can become muddy.

4 If the dye bath or container has a lid, put it on securely. Otherwise put the dye bath in a plastic bag and seal with clothes pegs (pins). Leave undisturbed for 24–48 hours, then remove the fabric and rinse thoroughly until the water is clear.

5 Wash in hot water with a little washing-up liquid added and then rinse again until the water runs clear. Allow fabrics to dry partially, then iron dry and air before using.

Making a solution for use with acid dyes

Acid-dyeing produces much more colourfast colours in silk than reactive dyeing. The dye is held in the fabric with acid – a vinegar. Make sure that the pans you use will not corrode.

Acid dyes will work only with the addition of an acid (such as white vinegar) to the dye bath. They are available as powder, which must be dissolved in boiling water, or in liquid form. They can be used on wool, alpaca, angora, cashmere and silk, but not on cotton or linen. The resulting colours are light-fast and will not bleach with washing. Always use a metal dye bath when working with acid dyes.

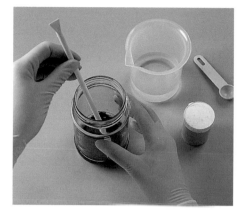

1 To make up a stock acid dye solution, pour 300ml/½ pint water into a jar, mark the level and pour it away. Measure 2.5ml/½ tsp dye powder into the jar and stir to a paste with a little cold water.

2 Add boiling water while stirring until the 300ml/½ pint mark is reached. This mixture will remain stable for several months.

Space-dyeing wool with acid dyes

Acid dyes work just as well on wool as they do on silk, and are excellent for dyeing knitting wool in hanks.

1 Weigh the material to be dyed. Soak it in warm water with a little washing-up (dishwashing) liquid added for at least 30 minutes. Squeeze out excess water gently, without wringing or rubbing. Crumple fabrics and place in the bottom of a metal pan, but lay skeins of yarn so that a maximum amount of the surface area is showing.

2 For each colour to be used, measure the volume of stock dye solution and pour it into a measuring beaker. Add any water necessary to make it up to the volume required. Pour the dyes carefully over the wool, aiming to cover all the white parts, and leave for 10 minutes. Use a maximum of 1½–2 times the volume of dye to fabric and yarn.

3 Add 1–3 times the volume of vinegar to fabric (more for deep colours) to water and pour in the side of the bath. Bring slowly to the boil. The dye should stay on the yarn: if the liquid is not clear, add vinegar. Simmer for 30 minutes. Remove from the heat and allow to cool. Rinse in hot water, adding cold water to cool the wool gradually. Squeeze out and dry.

Space-dyeing silk with acid dyes

Silk can be coloured with a glorious array of brightly coloured tones, muted shades and random patterns when dyed with acid dyes.

Acid-dyeing produces much faster colours in silk than reactive dyeing. The dye bath is heated to fix the dyes, but the silk must not boil or it will harden and crease badly. Using a water bath may make it easier to control the temperature.

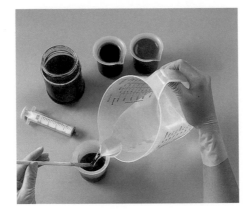

1 Weigh the silk then soak in warm water with a little washing-up (dishwashing) liquid added for at least 30 minutes. Squeeze out excess water and place fabric or yarn in the bottom of a metal pan.

2 For each colour to be used, measure the volume of stock dye solution and pour it into a measuring beaker. Add any water necessary to make it up to the volume required. Refer to the specific recipe.

3 Pour the dyes carefully over the silk. The total volume of dye should not be more than 1½–2 times the weight of the fabric or yarn: a larger amount may be used, but a flatter, more even colour will result.

4 Dye tends to colour silk quite fast, so make sure that all the white parts are covered. Leave for 10 minutes.

5 Use 1–3 times the volume of white vinegar to fabric, using more for deeper colours. Add the white vinegar to water and pour down the side of the dye bath so that it barely covers the fabric or yarn.

6 Heat the dye bath slowly to no more than 85°C/185°F, using a thermometer to check the temperature constantly. After 30 minutes at this temperature, remove from the heat and allow to cool before rinsing.

Fabric painting with reactive dyes

This permanent method of painting fabric can be used for many natural fabric types. Experiment with different painting tools.

1 Make 300ml/½ pint soda solution up to 1.5 litres/2¾ pints with water and immerse the prepared dry fabric for 10 minutes. Remove and allow to dry. Make up a solution of chemical water by dissolving 120g/4oz urea in 1 litre/1¾ pints hot water.

2 Measure 2.5ml/½ tsp dye into a small beaker. Add a few drops of cold water and stir to a paste. Add the chemical water slowly while stirring to make up the volume to 100ml/3½fl oz. Repeat for each colour used.

3 Arrange the fabric on a large plastic sheet to protect the work surface. Paint on the first colour with large brush strokes, evenly spaced over the surface. Wash the brush clean in cold water and allow to dry before changing colours.

4 Paint the subsequent colours evenly in the spaces, allowing some overlapping of the dye solutions. A smaller brush will give a more delicate effect and the dye solutions can be made up weaker if required.

5 Place a second sheet of plastic over the fabric and roll up around a length of plastic piping. Additional pieces of fabric can be rolled on top.

6 Put the roll inside another plastic bag and seal. Leave for 24–48 hours. Remove the fabric and rinse in cold water until it runs clear. Wash in hot soapy water and rinse again. Allow to dry partially, then iron dry.

Space-dye an assortment of rich fabrics together, using four shades of dye simultaneously, then assemble them into a traditional Victorian crazy patchwork design.

Crazy Patchwork Cushion

you will need

50cm/½yd white silk-satin, pre-washed

small amounts of textured silks, cotton and viscose fabrics (e.g. taffeta, beaded silk, brocade, cotton velvet)

short lengths of cotton lace

2m/2yd viscose cord

cold water reactive dyes, in blue, black, green and lemon yellow

washing soda (sodium carbonate)

dyeing equipment, including rubber gloves, plastic dye bath, jam jars, stirring rods, measuring beakers, plastic bag and clothes pegs (pins)

iron

ruler

lightweight calico

scissors

pencil

dressmaker's pins

needle

tacking (basting) thread

matching sewing thread

sewing machine

35cm/13½in zipper

40cm/16in square cushion pad

Recipe for 100g/3½oz fabric

• 50ml/2fl oz blue dye solution + 25ml/5 tsp soda solution

• 50ml/2fl oz black dye solution + 25ml/5 tsp soda solution

• 40ml/1½fl oz green + 20ml/4 tsp lemon yellow dye solutions + 30ml/1fl oz soda solution

• 25ml/5 tsp green + 25ml/5 tsp blue dye solutions + 25ml/5 tsp soda solution

1 Weigh the fabrics and adjust the recipe if necessary. Use solutions of 5ml/1 tsp dye in 300ml/½ pint hot water. Space-dye all the fabrics, lace and cord using the cold-water reactive dye method for deep colours.

2 Rinse and wash the dyed fabrics then iron dry. Leave the fabrics to air. Cut two 45cm/18in squares of lightweight calico. Mark the size of the cushion on one square in pencil, adding 2.5cm/1in seam allowance all round. Draw a 5cm/2in border inside the square, on both sides of the calico.

3 Cut a 43cm/17in square of the dyed silk-satin for the back of the cushion, and tack (baste) to the unmarked piece of calico. Trim the calico to size. Cut four strips of dyed silk-satin, each 7.5 x 44cm/3 x 17½in, and reserve for the borders.

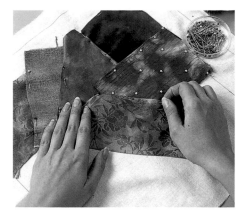

4 Cut pieces of the other dyed fabrics and position them in a random design on the centre square of the cushion front. Press under 5mm/¼in along the edges of the lighter fabrics and overlap them over the heavier fabrics. Overlap each patch by at least 1cm/½in. Pin in place.

5 Insert pieces of lace into some seams, hiding the raw ends under adjacent pieces of fabric. Neatly slip stitch the dyed patches to the calico backing, working from the centre outwards. Ensure that the patches remain flat and that there are no gaps.

6 Pin two of the borders, right sides down, to opposite sides of the patchwork. Stitch along the marked line with a 1cm/½in seam allowance. Press the borders outwards. Repeat with the other two borders. Trim the front to 43cm/17in square. Press under a small hem along one side of the front and the back. Insert the zipper. Pin, then stitch the remaining sides, leaving a 5mm/¼in gap near the zipper. Turn through and press. Slip stitch the dyed cord to the seamline and beside the zip on the front, inserting the knotted ends into the small gap. Slip stitch to close and insert the cushion pad.

These pretty little pyramid-shaped bags are made out of triangles of spray-dyed fabric, decorated with small beads and a ribbon loop for hanging over a coat-hanger.

Spray-dyed Lavender Bags

you will need

reactive dye solutions, in red, blue and violet, made up in chemical water

spray-dyeing equipment, including rubber gloves, spray bottles, measuring beakers and syringes

scraps of loosely-woven white cotton fabrics (e.g. cheesecloth or voile), pre-washed

paper and pencil

scissors

sewing machine

matching sewing thread

narrow ribbon

dried lavender

needle

small pearl beads

1 With your choice of colours spray-dye the fabric (see Techniques). Enlarge the template at the back of the book and cut out, marking the positions a, b, c, d, e and f. Using the template, cut out the fabric for the bags, matching the direction of the grain. One triangle makes one bag.

2 Leaving 5mm/¼in seam allowances throughout, fold point a to point b. Machine stitch down to d. Fold point c to meet point ab then stitch down to e. The fabric should now resemble a pyramid shape.

3 Fold a 10cm/4in length of ribbon into a loop. Pin the ends to align with the raw edges of the fabric at point abc, at the top of the pyramid. Pin and stitch down to point f. Turn the bag right side out.

4 Fill the bag loosely with lavender. Neatly slip stitch the opening closed.

5 Stitch small pearl beads around the base of the pyramid shape, securing the thread every three or four beads with a back stitch.

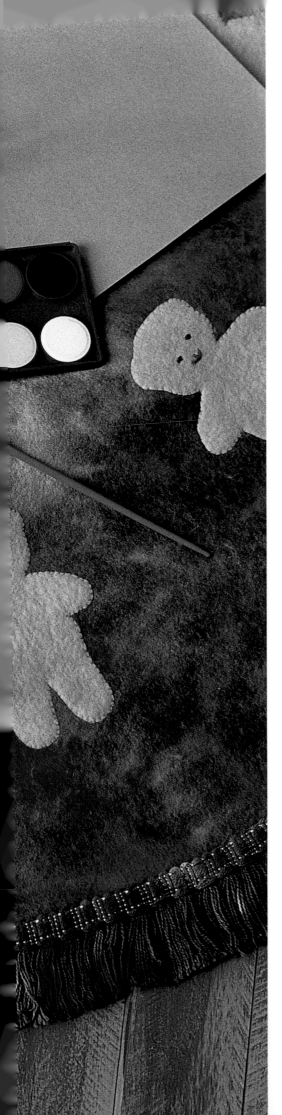

Here colourful space-dyed felt is appliquéd with teddy bears, also in space-dyed felt. The finished rug measures 90cm/36in diameter. Start with a large piece of felt as it could shrink by up to 30 per cent.

Teddy Bear Rug

you will need

1.4m/55in square of wool/viscose
felt for the rug, and 50 x 100cm/
20 x 40in for the teddy bears
cold water reactive dyes, in red, blue,
yellow and lemon yellow
washing soda (sodium carbonate)
dyeing equipment, including rubber
gloves, large plastic tray, measuring
beakers, glass jars and stirring rods
1m/1yd of 1.5m/59in-wide calico
iron
3m/3¼yd white cotton or viscose
fringe or braid
thin paper
tape measure
string
pencil
scissors
heavyweight iron-on interfacing
dressmaker's pins
glue stick
thin cardboard
craft knife and cutting mat
embroidery needle
stranded embroidery thread (floss)
needle
matching sewing thread
fusible bonding web
sewing machine

Recipe for 1.4m/55in square of felt, for the rug 320g/11½oz

• 210ml/7½fl oz red dye solution + 100ml/3½fl oz soda solution + water to make 350ml/12fl oz

• 185ml/6½fl oz blue dye solution + 90ml/3fl oz soda solution + water to make 350ml/12fl oz

• 160ml/5½fl oz yellow dye solution + 90ml/3fl oz soda solution + water to make 350ml/12fl oz

Recipe for 50 x 100cm/20 x 40in, for the bears (70g/2¼oz)

• 100ml/3½fl oz yellow dye solution + 40ml/1½fl oz soda solution

• 100ml/3½fl oz lemon yellow dye solution + 40ml/1½fl oz soda solution

Recipe for 1m/40in of 1.5m/59in-wide calico backing (240g/8½oz)

• 160ml/5½fl oz red dye solution + 75ml/2½fl oz soda solution + water to make 260ml/9½fl oz

• 140ml/4½fl oz blue dye solution + 70ml/2¼fl oz soda solution + water to make 260ml/9½fl oz

• 120ml/4fl oz yellow dye solution + 60ml/2fl oz soda solution + water to make 260ml/9½fl oz

1 Dye the felt for the rug and the teddy bears, using the cold-water reactive space-dyed method for deep colours (see Techniques). Use stock solutions of 2.5ml/½ tsp dye in 300ml/ ½ pint hot water. After dyeing and washing, the wool/viscose felt can be dried in a tumble drier.

2 Space-dye the calico and bias binding, using the same cold water method for deep colours. Wash and iron dry the calico. Space-dye the fringe or braid, using the same recipe, weighing the dry fringe and adjusting the amount of dye needed. If necessary, reshape the fringe while damp.

3 For the rug pattern, fold a 90cm/ 36in paper square into quarters. Hold the end of a 45cm/17¾in length of string in the folded corner, attach the other end to a pencil and draw a quarter circle. Cut out.

4 Using the opened paper pattern, cut out a circle of iron-on interfacing. Pin the interfacing web-side down on to the wrong side of the felt. Fuse the two together, working from the centre out . Cut off the excess felt.

5 Enlarge the teddy template provided, glue it on to cardboard and cut it out. Cut eight yellow felt teddies. Embroider the features.

6 Pin the teddies in a circle, 10cm/4in from the edge of the rug. Slip stitch each teddy to the rug. Iron the back of the rug.

▶**7** Cut one calico backing for the rug. Iron fusible web to the wrong side, cutting and piecing it to fit. Fuse the backing to the rug. Trim the edges.

8 Make 3m/3¼yd bias binding to go around the rug from dyed calico. Press under a 5mm/¼in seam down one long side and one short end of the binding.

9 Right sides together and raw edges aligned, pin the binding around the rug. Stitch, using a 1cm/½in seam allowance. Overlap the ends by 1cm/ ½in. Fold the binding over the edge of the rug and slip stitch it in place on the back. Press flat. On the front, slip stitch the fringe in place over the binding, folding under the raw ends.

Triangular flags, encrusted with beading and embroidery, and finished with tassels, form a distinctive window dressing. Team up with plain curtains dyed to match or use it alone to decorate a small window.

Paisley Pelmet

you will need

50cm/½yd of white cotton poplin

cold-water reactive dyes in yellow and lemon-yellow

washing soda (sodium carbonate)

dyeing equipment, including rubber gloves, plastic trays, glass jars, measuring beakers and syringes

small pieces of silk and cotton textured fabrics

tape measure

scissors

pencil and ruler

bonding powder and fusible web

unwoven pelmet stiffener

dressmaker's pins

baking paper (parchment paper)

iron

glue stick

thin and stiff cardboard

craft knife, rotary cutter and cutting mat

sewing machine

machine embroidery threads (floss), in shades of yellow and gold

embroidery and beading needles

yellow hand embroidery threads (floss), including gold thread

yellow and gold beads

shisha glass (optional)

matching sewing thread

length of 30 x 8mm/1¼ x ⅜in wooden batten, to fit across your window

Yellow recipe for 100g/3½ oz main fabric

• 150ml/5fl oz yellow dye solution + 60ml/2fl oz soda solution

• 150ml/5fl oz lemon-yellow dye solution + 60ml/2fl oz soda solution

Golden yellow recipe for 30g/1oz mixed fabrics

• 120ml/4fl oz yellow dye solution + 60ml/2fl oz soda solution

Lemon yellow recipe for 30g/1oz mixed fabrics

• 100ml/3½fl oz yellow dye solution + 60ml/2fl oz soda solution

1 Space-dye the poplin yellow using the cold water reactive dye method for deep colours (see Techniques). Use stock solutions of 2.5ml/½ tsp dye in 300ml/½ pint hot water. Dye small pieces of textured fabrics in two other shades of yellow.

2 Cut the batten casing from yellow poplin, 20cm/8in wide and as long as the batten, plus 3cm/1¼in all round for turnings. Set aside. Mark out a piece 10cm/4in wide and as long as the batten for the front of the batten, and as many 12 x 20cm/4¾ x 8in right-angled triangles as will fit across the window.

3 Bond the fabric for the flags and casing strip front to the pelmet stiffener using bonding powder. Sprinkle the powder over the stiffener, pin the poplin over the top and cover with baking paper (parchment paper) to protect the iron. Use a warm iron to bond the fabrics. Leave to cool.

4 Iron fusible bonding web to the wrong side of small pieces of the textured fabrics. Enlarge the paisley template from the back of the book to 4cm/1½in long. Glue on to thin cardboard and cut out using a craft knife or rotary cutter. Draw around the template on to the paper backing and cut out the fabric shapes.

5 Bond the shapes to the flags and central 3cm/1¼in of the casing strip, avoiding the pencil outlines. Using machine embroidery threads (floss), stitch gentle curved lines over and around the paisley shapes.

6 Decorate the flags with hand embroidery. Use chain stitch to surround the shapes and cable chain to stitch curvy lines.

7 Cut out the flags and trim the casing strip to 3cm/1¼in wide, using a rotary cutter. Add beads and shisha glass, if desired.

8 Cut an equal number of triangles from spare poplin. Pin each decorated flag to a backing piece then machine stitch around the edge with a small, narrow zigzag stitch.

9 Fold the reserved batten casing in half lengthways and press. Turn under and press 1.5cm/⅝in at each short end. Pin the decorated casing strip 3mm/⅛in from the foldline and stitch with a narrow zigzag. Pin the casing loosely around the batten. Remove the batten and stitch along the pinned line. Stitch the flags securely to the casing, just under the previous seam. Press the raw edges of the casing up, insert the batten then slip stitch the raw edges in place.

10 To make the tassels, cut two pieces of thick cardboard 7cm/2¾in square. Wind silk thread around the cards until the tassel is fat enough, then push a needle and thread between them at the top and tie tightly.

11 Cut the loops at the bottom between the cards. Wind double thread around each tassel about 1.5cm/⅝in from the top, thread the ends through the loop, pull tight and tie. Trim the bottom. Stitch one tassel to the end of each flag.

In this lovely design, inspired by Monet's paintings of water-lilies, it is the embroidery threads that are space-dyed. Two kinds of thread are used to give a textured effect.

Embroidered Pincushion

you will need

20cm/8in square of canvas, 10 threads to 2.5cm/1in

plastic sheet

masking tape

medium artist's paintbrush

fabric paints, in green, sapphire blue and light pink

iron

10g/¼oz white silk 4-ply thread

25cm/10in square of white silk-satin

acid dyes, in bright pinky-red, violet, green and reddish-blue

white vinegar

dyeing equipment, including rubber gloves, metal bowls, measuring spoons, glass jars, stirring rod and thermometer

50g/2oz 4-ply white wool (yarn)

paper and pencil

scissors

dressmaker's pins

felt-tipped pen

ruler

needle

tacking (basting) thread

embroidery needles

25cm/10in square of lightweight calico

sewing machine

matching sewing thread

polyester toy stuffing

thick cardboard

Recipe for the silk thread and silk-satin

• 40ml/1½fl oz dilute pinky-red dye solution

• 20ml/4 tsp dilute violet dye solution

• 40ml/1½fl oz dilute green dye solution

Recipe for 4-ply wool (yarn)

• 5ml/1 tsp reddish-blue dye solution + 60ml /2fl oz water

• 10ml/2 tsp green dye solution + 60ml/2fl oz water

• 5ml/1 tsp violet dye solution + 60ml/2fl oz water

1 Space-dye the silk thread and the silk-satin with acid dyes, using the method for silk described in Techniques. Use stock solutions of 2.5ml/½ tsp dye in 300ml/½ pint boiling water, diluted by making 20ml/4 tsp dye solution up to 100ml/3½fl oz with water. Iron the silk-satin dry and hang the thread up to dry.

3 Space-dye 50g/2oz 4-ply wool (yarn) using the method for wool described in Techniques. Use stock solutions of 2.5ml/½ tsp dye in 300ml/½ pint boiling water. Leave to dry thoroughly. Enlarge the template provided to the required size. Cut it out. Pin the paper template to the canvas and draw around it using a felt-tipped pen and ruler. Stitch over the marked lines using tacking (basting) thread.

2 Place the canvas on the plastic and secure with tape. Brush green paint evenly over the whole canvas. Add areas of sapphire blue. Cover any remaining areas with pink. Leave to dry for 24 hours. Iron the canvas on the wrong side to fix (set) the dye.

4 Using two strands of dyed silk thread, fill in the central square of the design area with random long stitch. Work the stitches in varying lengths along each row. Work one row from left to right, then the next row from right to left.

5 Using two strands of wool, work the outer shapes in random long stitch, keeping the top and bottom lines and the diagonal lines as straight edges. Tack the calico to the wrong side of the silk. Pin the silk and canvas right sides together. Stitch around three sides into the last row of stitches.

6 Trim the seams, clip the corners and turn through to the right side. Stuff with toy filling (stuffing), then tuck in the seam allowances along the open side. Do not make the pincushion too fat. Neatly slip stitch the opening closed, leaving about 5mm/¼in open at one end.

7 Make a twisted cord from two strands of wool and one of silk. Tie the three ends to a fixed point and twist together. Fold in half, hold the ends and the two lengths will twist together. Knot the two ends together. Tuck the knot into the opening. Couch the cord around the pincushion seam. As you approach the end, re-tie the knot to make it fit exactly and tuck it inside the seam. Stitch the opening.

8 To make the tassels, wind dyed silk around a 4cm/1½in square of cardboard. Push a needle threaded with a length of silk between the pieces of cardboard and knot tightly. Cut the loops at the bottom of the tassel. Double another piece of silk and thread a needle. Wind around the tassel about 1.5cm/⅝in from the top, thread the ends through the loop and pull tight. Stitch into this thread several times to secure. Make four tassels. Trim, then stitch one to each corner.

Painting reactive dyes on to sheer fabric creates a soft, pretty effect even when the colours are vibrant. This practical drawstring bag is lined with waterproof shower fabric.

Dye-painted Cosmetic Bag

you will need

0.5m/½yd cotton lawn or poplin, pre-washed

2m/2yd thick cotton piping cord

cold water reactive dyes, in red, yellow and blue

urea and washing soda (sodium carbonate)

dyeing equipment, including rubber gloves, measuring spoons, beakers and stirring rods

small decorator's paintbrush

plastic sheets, plastic piping, plastic bag and clothes pegs (pins)

small plastic box

iron

tape measure

scissors

50cm/½yd shower curtain fabric

sewing machine

matching sewing thread

dressmaker's pins

needle

tacking (basting) thread

large safety pin

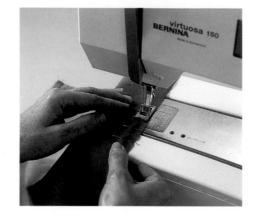

1 Colour the fabric and the piping cord using the painting with reactive dyes method (see Techniques). Put the cord in a small plastic box for 48 hours. Wash the fabric and iron dry.

3 Press under 5mm/¼in around the top edge of the bag, then turn down and press a 9cm/3½in hem. Turn the bag right side out.

2 Cut one piece 75 x 27cm/30 x 11in and a piece of shower curtain fabric 55 x 27cm/22 x 11in, for the lining. Fold the lining in half and machine stitch the side seams, leaving a 1cm/½in seam allowance. Fold the dyed fabric in half and stitch both side seams down to 15cm/6in from the top. Leave a 2cm/¾in gap, then stitch to the bottom. Press the side seams open.

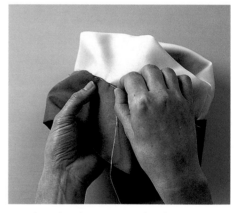

4 Slip the lining inside the bag and tuck it under the hem. Pin the bottom of the hem, then turn the bag inside out and tack (baste) close to the edge. Turn the bag right side out. Using matching thread, machine stitch along the tacking line. To make a casing for the piping, add two more rows of stitching, 7cm/2¾in and 5cm/2in from the top, to correspond with the side seam gaps.

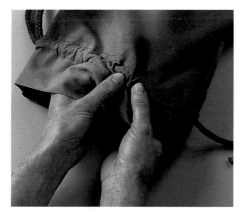

5 Turn the bag inside out and catch the lining to the bag at the lower corners with one or two stitches. Turn the bag right side out and press lightly, ensuring that the heat of the iron does not melt the shower curtain fabric. Cut two lengths of piping cord, each 80cm/32in. Attach a safety pin to one end of one cord and thread through a side opening, around the casing and return to the same opening. Repeat with the second cord through the other opening. Knot the ends.

Stitch pennant-shaped triangles of vibrant contrast-dyed fabric around this deep blue tablecloth. These instructions are for a cloth 1.40m/55in square, but you can adjust the size to fit your table.

Party Tablecloth

you will need

tape measure

scissors

3.7m/4yd of 1.5m/59in-wide cotton poplin, pre-washed

cold-water reactive dyes in blue, reddish-blue, black, yellow, lemon-yellow, red, violet and green

washing soda (sodium carbonate)

dyeing equipment, including rubber gloves, plastic trays and bags, glass jars, measuring spoons and beakers

iron

paper and pencil

ruler

tailor's chalk

sewing machine

multi-coloured machine embroidery thread (floss)

matching sewing threads

needle

tacking (basting) thread

dressmaker's pins

Recipes

Dark blue

• 540ml/19fl oz blue dye solution + 180ml/6fl oz soda solution

• 540ml/19fl oz reddish-blue dye solution + 180ml/6fl oz soda solution

• 180ml/6fl oz black dye solution + 90ml/3fl oz soda solution

Yellow

• 75ml/2½fl oz yellow dye solution + 40ml/1½fl oz soda solution + 75ml 2½fl oz water

• 75ml/2½fl oz lemon-yellow dye solution + 40ml/1½fl oz soda solution + 75ml/2½fl oz water

Deep pink

• 150ml/5fl oz red dye solution + 70ml/2¼fl oz soda solution

• 75ml/2½fl oz violet dye solution + 40ml/1½fl oz soda solution

Green

• 30ml/1fl oz yellow + 120ml/4fl oz green dye solutions + 75ml/2½fl oz soda solution

• 50ml/2fl oz yellow + 100ml/3½fl oz blue dye solutions + 75ml/2½fl oz soda solution

1 Cut the poplin into four lengths: 2.25m/2½yd for the dark blue tablecloth, bindings and triangles, and three pieces 50cm/20in long for the contrast colours. Space-dye the fabric, using the reactive dye method for deep colours (see Techniques) and stock solutions of 5ml/1 tsp dye in 300ml/½ pint hot water throughout. Fix (set) the colours.

2 Enlarge the triangle template provided to measure 20cm/8in long, plus 1cm/½in seam allowances. Cut 14 triangles in each of the four colours. Cut four strips 5cm x 1.5m/2 x 59in in blue to bind the edge of the cloth.

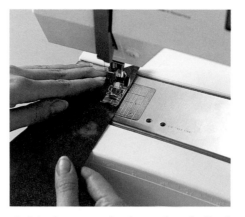

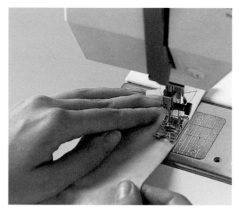

3 Using tailor's chalk, mark a diamond grid on the tablecloth, spacing the lines 20cm/8in apart. Draw the first line diagonally from corner to corner, then work the lines from the centre outwards.

4 Machine stitch along the chalked lines, using multi-coloured machine embroidery thread (floss) and straight stitch. Leaving a 1cm/½in seam allowance and using matching threads, stitch each pair of triangles together along the two bias edges.

5 Trim the corners and turn through, pushing the point of the triangle out, and press. Top stitch close to each edge using multi-coloured thread. Tack (baste) together the unstitched edges of each triangle. There will be seven triangles in each colour.

6 Right sides together, pin and tack the raw edge of the triangles to the edge of the cloth, pointing inwards, lining them up with the stitched grid. Maintain the colour sequence red, yellow, green, blue.

Press under 1cm/½in along one long edge of the bindings. With right sides together and raw edges aligned, pin the binding to two opposite edges of the cloth. Stitch in place.

Press the binding to the wrong side and slip stitch the turned-under edge in place, covering the raw edges of the triangles. Repeat for the other two sides. Top stitch the edge of the tablecloth in a contrast colour.

For a floating summer window dressing, space-dye muslin (cheese-cloth) using the method for pale colours to give pastel shades. Decorate it with machine-stitched lines and tiny beads.

Delicate Muslin Curtain

you will need

curtain-weight muslin (cheesecloth) to fit window, allowing 15cm/6in per drop for hems and casings, plus shrinkage, pre-washed

cold-water reactive dyes, in red, blue, lemon yellow and green

washing soda (sodium carbonate)

dyeing equipment, including rubber gloves, measuring spoons, beakers, glass jars, stirring rods and large plastic tray

iron and thick towel

scissors

multi-coloured machine embroidery thread (floss)

sewing machine

matching sewing thread

fine needle

small pearl and/or glass beads

Recipe for 2.5m/2¾yd of muslin

• 19ml/4 tsp red dye solution + 40ml/1½fl oz soda solution + water to make 250ml/9fl oz

• 19ml/4 tsp blue dye solution + 40ml/1½fl oz soda solution + water to make 250ml/9fl oz

• 8ml/1½ tsp lemon yellow + 12ml/2½ tsp green dye solutions + 40ml/1½fl oz soda solution + water to make 250ml/9fl oz

1 Space-dye the muslin, using the cold water reactive method for pale colours described (see Techniques). Use stock dye solutions of 2.5ml/½ tsp dye in 300ml/½ pint hot water. Wash the fabric and iron dry. Trim the side edges, then fold in half lengthways. Working on one-quarter of the curtain at a time, press lengthways folds 3–4cm/1¼–½in apart.

2 Using multi-coloured embroidery thread (floss), machine stitch along the pressed lines. Begin stitching at varying distances from the top and stitch to the bottom of the curtain. Start each row with a few reverse stitches. Cut the bobbin thread at the top, but leave the front thread hanging. Press the curtain.

3 Using matching thread, stitch a 5cm/2in double hem at the base of the curtain, and a 2.5cm/1in casing at the top. Thread a fine needle with the loose thread at the top of each row and attach a bead. Add further beads at random intervals down each row. Press lightly on the wrong side, resting the curtain on a thick towel. Check that the heat of the iron will not melt the beads.

In this brightly coloured bag, two dyeing methods are used – the pepperpot method of sprinkling dye, and space-dyeing. With each method, dye extra fabric and choose the best pieces for the patchwork.

Patchwork Toy Bag

you will need

1.5m/59in-wide white cotton lawn

2.50m/2¾yd cotton piping cord

cold-water reactive dyes in red, green and violet

salt

washing soda (sodium carbonate)

dyeing equipment, including rubber gloves, plastic trays, measuring beakers, jam jars, plastic bag, clothes pegs (pins), pepperpots (pepper shakers) or muslin squares and household paintbrush

scissors

pencil and ruler

rotary cutter and cutting mat

dressmaker's pins

sewing machine

matching sewing threads

iron

large safety pin

Recipe for deep pink

• 400ml/14fl oz red dye solution + 200ml/7fl oz soda solution

1 Space-dye at least four pieces of lawn by the pepperpot (pepper shaker) method using red, green and violet dyes (see Techniques,). Dye 1m/40in lawn and the piping cord deep pink by the reactive space-dyeing method for deep colours (see Techniques). The recipe given is for about 150g/5½oz fabric and cord. Use a stock solution of 5ml/1 tsp dye in 300ml/½ pint hot water. From pepperpot fabric, cut 24 squares, each 12cm/4¾in. From deep pink, cut 24 squares and two pieces 62 x 42cm/24½ x 16½in for the lining.

2 Leaving 1cm/½in seams, pin the squares together in rows, alternating the colours. Machine stitch, then press the seams to one side. Make 12 rows of four squares each.

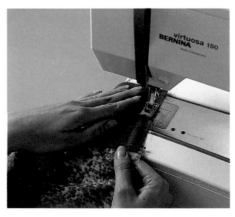

3 Stitch six rows together for each side, alternating the colours. Trim the extra fabric from the corners, then press the seams to one side.

4 Right sides together, pin and stitch both long sides of the lining pieces together, leaving a 1cm/½in seam, to make a tube. Press the seams open. Repeat with the two patchwork pieces, leaving a 3cm/1¼in gap in each side seam 7cm/2¾in from the top. Press the seams open.

5 With right sides together and side seams matching, slip one tube inside the other. Stitch together around the top, through two layers of fabric. Turn through and press. Top stitch on the outside of the bag. Form the casing for the cord with two rows of machine stitching parallel to the top edge and 7cm/2¾in and 10cm/4in below it.

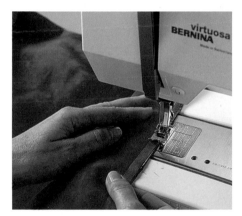

6 Turn the bag inside out and stitch the bottom through all four layers of fabric. Stitch again to reinforce the seam. Trim the bottom edges and tidy with zigzag stitch. Turn through to the right side.

7 Cut the piping cord in half. Attach a safety pin to the end of one piece and thread through a side opening, around the casing and out through the same opening. Repeat with the second piece of cord through the second side opening. Knot all of the ends to finish.

Templates

Above and right: *Cross Stitch Monograms,*
p72–3

Below: *Elizabethan Pattern
Lampshade,* p52

Mexican Motif Place Mats, p44

Sponge-printed Gingham Bed Linen, p38–9

Summery Duvet Cover, p46–7

Wild Rose Chiffon Scarf, p70–1

Fish-stencilled Shower Curtain,
p53

Patterned Seat Cover, p106–7

Stars-and-stripes Floorcloth,
p106–7

Mosaic Stencilled Tablecloth, p50–1

Foam-printed Boat Towel, p42–3

Stained Glass Panel, p102–3

Stencilled Quilt, p48–9

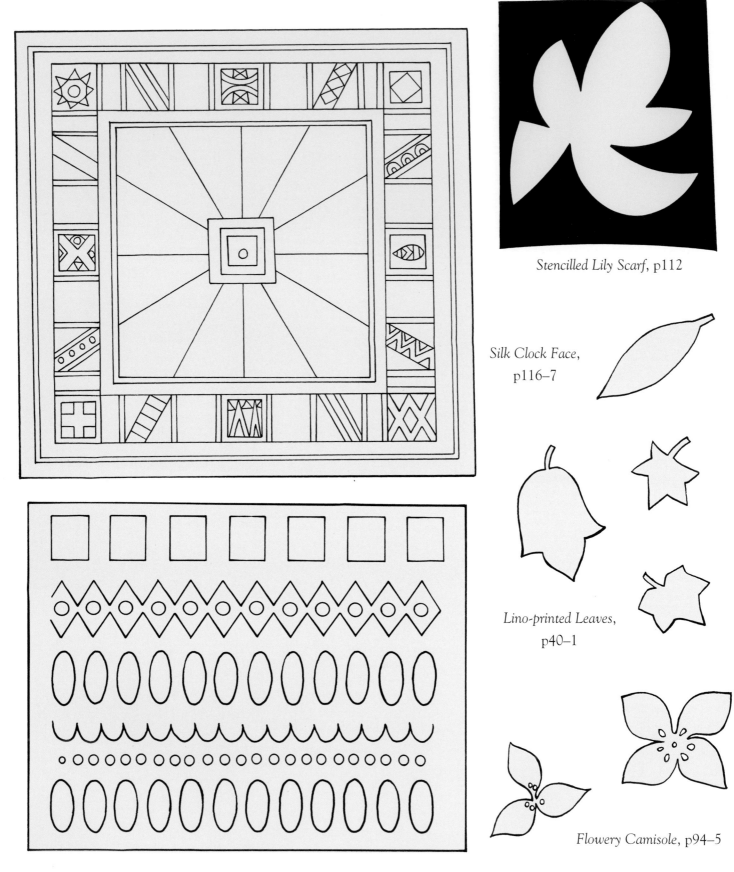

Stencilled Lily Scarf, p112

Silk Clock Face, p116–7

Lino-printed Leaves, p40–1

Flowery Camisole, p94–5

Crackled Scarf, p134–5

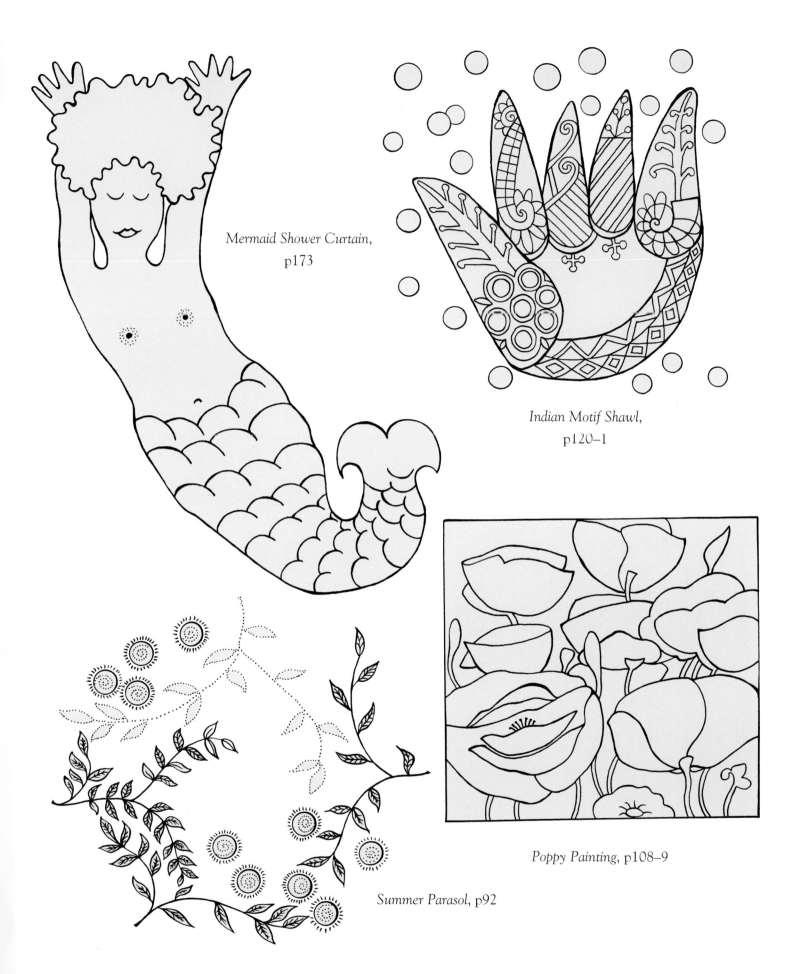

Mermaid Shower Curtain,
p173

Indian Motif Shawl,
p120–1

Poppy Painting, p108–9

Summer Parasol, p92

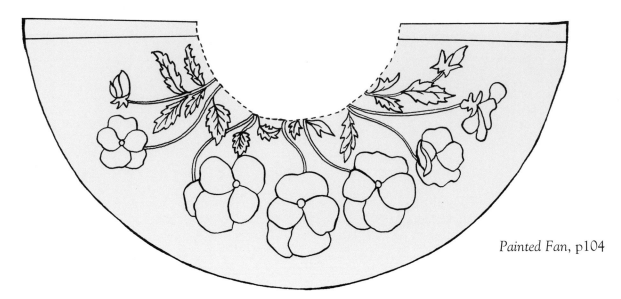

Painted Fan, p104

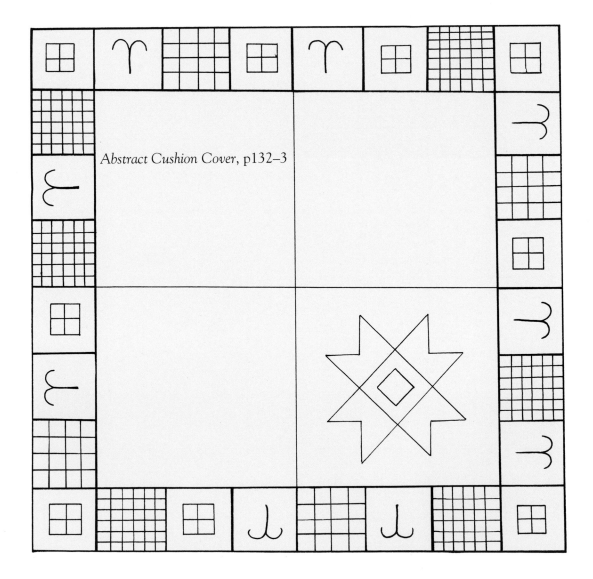

Abstract Cushion Cover, p132–3

Above: *Maple Leaf Table Runner* p156–7
Enlarge by 200% for exact size

Left: *Cotton Sarong* p140–1
Enlarge by 200% for exact size

Modern Painting p138–9
Enlarge by 400% for exact size

Bordered Scarf p152–3
Enlarge by 200% for exact size

Quilted Table Mat p160–1
Enlarge by 250% for exact size

Tiger Deckchair, p146–7
Enlarge by 500% for exact size

Square Silk Scarf, p162–3
Enlarge to 37.5cm/15in square for exact size

Silk Velvet Scarf,
p142–3
Enlarge by 200%
for exact size

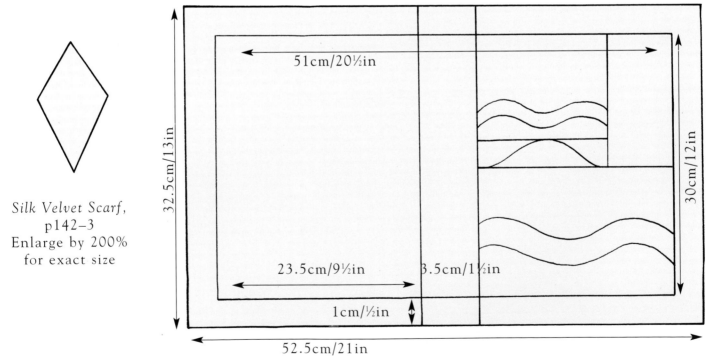

51cm/20½in

32.5cm/13in

30cm/12in

23.5cm/9½in   3.5cm/1½in

1cm/½in

52.5cm/21in

Leather Book Cover, p136–7

Teddy Bear Rug, p228–30
Enlarge to 14cm/5½in high

Velvet Blind, p182–3. Enlarge by 300% for exact size

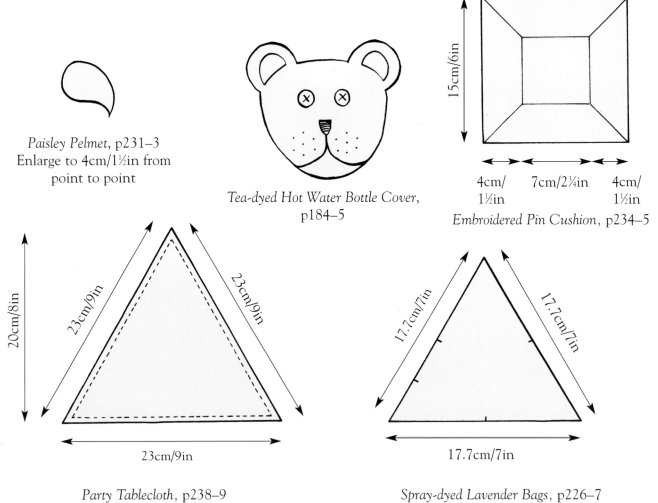

Paisley Pelmet, p231–3
Enlarge to 4cm/1½in from
point to point

Tea-dyed Hot Water Bottle Cover,
p184–5

Embroidered Pin Cushion, p234–5

15cm/6in

4cm/
1½in   7cm/2¾in   4cm/
1½in

20cm/8in

23cm/9in   23cm/9in

23cm/9in

Party Tablecloth, p238–9

17.7cm/7in   17.7cm/7in

17.7cm/7in

Spray-dyed Lavender Bags, p226–7

Index

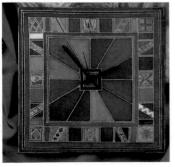

Acknowledgements

The publisher would like to thank the following people for designing projects in this book:

Ofer Acoo for the Sunflower Cushion Cover p113.

Petra Boase for the Stamped Calico Blind p26–7, Diamond-printed Director's Chair p30–1, Feather-printed Muslin Curtain p32–3, Leaf Print Table Runner p34–5 and Flower Pot Throw p62–3.

Penny Boylan for the Velvet-edged Throw p178–9 and Tea-dyed Hot Water Bottle Cover p184–5.

Stephanie Donaldson for the Mermaid Shower Curtain p173.

Lucinda Ganderton for the Foam-printed Boat Towel p42–3, Abstract Picture Frame p114–5, Tie-dyed Jewellery Roll p176–7 and Marbled Spectacle Case p196–7.

Elaine Green for the Vinegar-glazed Floorcloth p80–1.

Judith Gussin for the Block-printed Chair Pad p22–3, Crazy Patchwork Cushion p224–5, Spray-dyed Lavender Bags p226–7, Teddy Bear Rug p228–30, Paisley Pelmet p231–3, Dye-painted Cosmetic Bag, p236–7, Party Tablecloth p238–9 and Patchwork Toy Bag p69.

Sheila Gussin for designing the Teddy Bear Rug p228–30, for the Embroidered Pin Cushion p234–5, and Delicate Muslin Curtain p240–1.

Helen Heery for the Cotton Sarong p140–1, Silk Velvet Scarf p142–3, Striped Silk Tie p158–9 and Silk Square Scarf p162–3.

Karin Hossack for the Sponge-printed Gingham Bed Linen p38–9, Cross-stitch Monograms p72–3 and Doughnut Floor Cushion p186–7.

Alison Jenkins for the Fruit-printed Blind and Curtains p36–7, Mexican Printed Place Mats p44, Mosaic Stencilled Tablecloth p50–1, Marbled Fabric Desk Set p192–3 and Folded Napkin Parcels p208–9.

Sipra Majumder for the Leather Book Cover p136–7.

Wendy Massey for the Pet's Bow Tie p64.

Sarbjitt Natt for the Zodiac Scarf p105 and Silk Clock Face p116–17.

Sandra Partington for the Elizabethan Pattern Lampshade p52, Checked Café Curtain p75, Stained Glass Panel p102–3, Stencilled Lily Scarf p112 and Marbled Drawstring Bag p194–5.

Isabel Stanley for the Leaf-painted Organza Scarf p65, Summer Parasol p92, Flowery Camisole p94–5, Polka Dot Kite p98, Resist-spotted Sarong p99, Patterned Seat Cover p106–7, Indian Motif Shawl p120–1 and Marbled Book Cover p200–1.

Susie Stokoe for the Lino-printed Leaves p 40–1, Summery Duvet Cover p46–7, Fish-stencilled Shower Curtain p53, Multi-textured Lampshade p78–79, Abstract Shawl p96–7, Salt-painted Tie p100–1, Painted Fan p104, Poppy Painting p108–9, Salt-patterned Greeting Card p110–11, Crackled Scarf p134–5, Modern Painting p138–9, Crackle-finish Cosmetic Bag p144–5, Tiger Deckchair p146–7, Lightweight Folding Screen p148–9, Chequered Cushion Cover p150–1, Bordered Scarf p152–3, Geometric Napkin p154–5, Maple Leaf Table Runner p156–7, Quilted Table Mat p160–1, Dip-dyed Lampshade p174–5, Tassel-edged Lampshade p180–1, Velvet Blind p182–3, Double-dyed Place Mats p188–9, Folded Silk Handkerchiefs p190–1, Pleated Table Runner p202–3, Tie-dye Duvet Cover p204–5 and Tie-dyed Patchwork Cushion p206–7.

Liz Wagstaff for the Block-printed Velvet Cushion p45.

Stewart and Sally Walton for the Stamped Bed Linen Borders p24, Autumnal Floor Cushions p25, Potato-printed Tablecloth p28–9, Stencilled Quilt p48–9 and Stars-and-Stripes Floorcloth p66–7.

Dorothy Wood for the Abstract Cushion Cover p132–3.